AF572027

Bible Promises to Treasure *for Newlyweds*

Bible Promises to Treasure *for Newlyweds*

Inspiring

words

for every

occasion

Nashville, Tennessee

Bible Promises to Treasure for Newly Marrieds

Nashville, Tennessee

Printed in Belgium

ISBN 0–8054–9391–3

Dewey Decimal Classification: 248.8
Subject Heading: SPOUSES

******

A note on the sources of quotations. When possible I have supplied at least the book name from which contemporary quotes have come. Yet even this is often impossible, since many came from my "journal of jottings" over many years. Also, if a quote is from a person who lived longer than fifty or so years ago, I've made no attempt to cite the source. Such quotations are usually available in any standard book of quotes.

******

Library of Congress Cataloging-in-Publication Data

Bible promises to treasure for newly marrieds: inspiring words for every occasion / compiled by Gary Wilde.

p. cm.

Includes bibliographical references.

ISBN 0–8054–9391–3

1. Spouses—Religious life. I. Wilde, Gary

BV4596.M3B55 1999

248'.8 —dc21 99–28251

CIP

1 2 3 4 5 6 03 02 01 00 99

S

Contents

—8—

Money Matters 150

—9—

Are You Ready for Parenting? 159

—10—

Let's Make This Marriage Work 177

Introduction

I remember as a child singing often at church: "Standing on the Promises of God." Or maybe it was mostly the adults who were singing; but I was standing next to them—my parents and all the others. I recall those faithful people joyfully reciting words they must surely have known by heart . . .

When the howling storms
of doubt and fear assail,
By the living Word of God I shall prevail,
Standing on the promises of God.

For years Downey Church, in sunny central Florida, had preached and taught the promises of God and believed in His goodness. From the beginning—when the church building was a small tin-roofed, A-frame at the east end of a dirt road on the outskirts of Orlando—people would gather to stand on the immutable promises. Under the shiny tin roof, standing on the sandy-wooden floorboards, they melded their voices to the tunes of the upright piano and recalled God's goodness. Today, as the church there grows and thrives—now there is also a school and gymnasium—I can only attribute its vibrant life to a love of God's promises and the recognition that without the pledges that flow from the mouth of God, there is no church, no music, and no reason for either.

The promises of God have always been the bedrock of Christian faith; for without God's sacred covenants with us, we cannot survive. In times of joy or heartache, in all our ups and downs, we keep coming back to that source of our life: the motivation for all our doing and the reason for our existence. It is the message of God's mighty assurances: this life is not all there is, He will always be with us while we are here, and He will take us to be with Him someday. Yes, we do have priceless promises to keep close to our hearts!

My hope for you as you delve into this scriptural treasure chest is that you will grow deeper in love with the One who has spoken as no other ever could. With so many influences bombarding our minds each moment of the day, what could be better than to set aside a few moments of quiet to hear the still, small voice that constantly invites us into warm fellowship? We'll be richly rewarded if we truly listen to what that voice is saying. His words convey blessing and guidance, wisdom and warning, life for now and life everlasting. What incomparable grace!

Gary Wilde

Oviedo, Florida, 1999

—One—

Ready for Your New Role?

Who are you? How many hats do you wear in one day? Now it's time to add one more. But this new role must take priority over all the others, bringing them together and shaping them into a new lifestyle that carries significant responsibilities, as well as exciting new dreams and goals, all shared with a partner who loves you deeply.

You Both Have New Responsibilities

It takes two to make a marriage a success and only one to make it a failure.

—Herbert Samuel

Submitting yourselves one to another in the fear of God.

—Ephesians 5:21

❤ *Trust the Lord to Supply*

Therefore I say unto you, Take no thought for your life, what ye shall eat, or what ye shall drink; nor yet for your body, what ye shall put on. Is not the life more than meat, and the body than raiment?

Behold the fowls of the air: for they sow not, neither do they reap, nor gather into barns; yet your heavenly Father feedeth them. Are ye not much better than they?

Which of you by taking thought can add one cubit unto his stature?

And why take ye thought for raiment? Consider the lilies of the field, how they grow; they toil not, neither do they spin:

And yet I say unto you, That even Solomon in all his glory was not arrayed like one of these.

Wherefore, if God so clothe the grass of the field, which to day is, and to morrow is cast into the oven, shall he not much more clothe you, O ye of little faith?

Therefore take no thought, saying, What shall we eat? or, What shall we drink? or, Wherewithal shall we be clothed?

(For after all these things do the Gentiles seek:) for your heavenly Father knoweth that ye have need of all these things.

But seek ye first the kingdom of God, and his righteousness; and all these things shall be added unto you.

Take therefore no thought for the morrow: for the morrow shall take thought for the things of itself. Sufficient unto the day is the evil thereof.

—Matthew 6:25–34

Be careful for nothing; but in every thing by prayer and supplication with thanksgiving let your requests be made known unto God.

—*Philippians 4:6*

❤ *Learn Selfless Cooperation*

Bear ye one another's burdens, and so fulfil the law of Christ.

—*Galatians 6:2*

Again I say unto you, That if two of you shall agree on earth as touching any thing that they shall ask, it shall be done for them of my Father which is in heaven.

For where two or three are gathered together in my name, there am I in the midst of them.

—*Matthew 18:19–20*

For I came down from heaven, not to do mine own will, but the will of him that sent me.

—*John 6:38*

Let this mind be in you, which was also in Christ Jesus.

—Philippians 2:5

❤ *Avoid Any Form of Deceitfulness*

Ye shall not steal, neither deal falsely, neither lie one to another.

—Leviticus 19:11

Lie not one to another, seeing that ye have put off the old man with his deeds;

And have put on the new man, which is renewed in knowledge after the image of him that created him.

—Colossians 3:9–10

Remove from me the way of lying: and grant me thy law graciously.

I have chosen the way of truth: thy judgments have I laid before me.

I have stuck unto thy testimonies: O LORD, put me not to shame.

I will run the way of thy commandments, when thou shalt enlarge my heart.

Teach me, O LORD, the way of thy statutes; and I shall keep it unto the end.

Give me understanding, and I shall keep thy law; yea, I shall observe it with my whole heart.

Make me to go in the path of thy commandments; for therein do I delight.

Incline my heart unto thy testimonies, and not to covetousness.

Turn away mine eyes from beholding vanity; and quicken thou me in thy way.

—Psalm 119: 29–37

Husbands: Love Your Wives

A wife is a gift bestowed upon man to reconcile him to the loss of paradise.

—Johann von Goethe

Husbands, love your wives, even as Christ also loved the church, and gave himself for it;

That he might sanctify and cleanse it with the washing of water by the word,

That he might present it to himself a glorious church, not having spot, or wrinkle, or any such thing; but that it should be holy and without blemish.

So ought men to love their wives as their own bodies. He that loveth his wife loveth himself.

For no man ever yet hated his own flesh; but nourisheth and cherisheth it, even as the Lord the church:

For we are members of his body, of his flesh, and of his bones.

For this cause shall a man leave his father and mother, and shall be joined unto his wife, and they two shall be one flesh.

This is a great mystery: but I speak concerning Christ and the church.

Nevertheless, let every one of you in particular so love his wife even as himself; and the wife see that she reverence her husband.

—Ephesians 5:25–33

Likewise, ye husbands, dwell with them according to knowledge, giving honour unto the wife, as unto the weaker vessel, and as being heirs together of the grace of life; that your prayers be not hindered.

—1 Peter 3:7

❤ *Follow Faithful Men Like These*

Isaac

And Isaac came from the way of the well Lahai-roi; for he dwelt in the south country.

And Isaac went out to meditate in the field at the eventide: and he lifted up his eyes, and saw, and, behold, the camels were coming.

And Rebekah lifted up her eyes, and when she saw Isaac, she lighted off the camel.

For she had said unto the servant, What man is this that walketh in the field to meet us? And the servant had said, It is my master: therefore she took a vail, and covered herself.

And the servant told Isaac all things that he had done.

And Isaac brought her into his mother Sarah's tent, and took Rebekah, and she became his wife; and he loved her.

—Genesis 24:62–67a

Joseph, The Husband of Mary

Now the birth of Jesus Christ was on this wise: When as his mother Mary was espoused to Joseph, before they came together, she was found with child of the Holy Ghost.

Then Joseph her husband, being a just man, and not willing to make her a publick example, was minded to put her away privily.

But while he thought on these things, behold, the angel of the Lord appeared unto him in a dream, saying, Joseph, thou son of David, fear not to take unto thee Mary thy wife: for that which is conceived in her is of the Holy Ghost.

And she shall bring forth a son, and thou shalt call his name JESUS: for he shall save his people from their sins.

Now all this was done, that it might be fulfilled which was spoken of the Lord by the prophet, saying,

Behold, a virgin shall be with child, and shall bring forth a son, and they shall call his name Emmanuel, which being interpreted is, God with us.

Then Joseph being raised from sleep did as the angel of the Lord had bidden him, and took unto him his wife:

And knew her not till she had brought forth her firstborn son: and he called his name JESUS.

—*Matthew 1:18–25*

Wives: Honor Your Husbands

Of all the home remedies, a good wife is best.

—*Kin Hubbard*

Likewise, ye wives, be in subjection to your own husbands; that, if any obey not the word, they also may without the word be won by the conversation of the wives;

While they behold your chaste conversation coupled with fear.

Whose adorning let it not be that outward adorning of plaiting the hair, and of wearing of gold, or of putting on of apparel;

But let it be the hidden man of the heart, in that which is not corruptible, even the ornament of a meek and quiet spirit, which is in the sight of God of great price.

For after this manner in the old time the holy women also, who trusted in God, adorned themselves, being in subjection unto their own husbands:

Even as Sara obeyed Abraham, calling him lord: whose daughters ye are, as long as ye do well, and are not afraid with any amazement.

—1 Peter 3:1–6

❤ *Seek the Character of These Godly Women*

HANNAH

Now there was a certain man of Ramathaimzophim, of mount Ephraim, and his name was Elkanah, the son of Jeroham, the son of Elihu, the son of Tohu, the son of Zuph, an Ephrathite:

And he had two wives; the name of the one was Hannah, and the name of the other Peninnah: and Peninnah had children, but Hannah had no children.

And this man went up out of his city yearly to worship and to sacrifice unto the LORD of hosts in Shiloh. And the two sons of Eli, Hophni and Phinehas, the priests of the LORD, were there.

And when the time was that Elkanah offered, he gave to Peninnah his wife, and to all her sons and her daughters, portions:

But unto Hannah he gave a worthy portion; for he loved Hannah: but the LORD had shut up her womb.

And her adversary also provoked her sore, for to make her fret, because the LORD had shut up her womb.

And as he did so year by year, when she went up to the house of the LORD, so she provoked her; therefore she wept, and did not eat.

Then said Elkanah her husband to her, Hannah, why weepest thou? and why eatest thou not? and why is thy heart grieved? am not I better to thee than ten sons?

So Hannah rose up after they had eaten in Shiloh, and after they had drunk. Now Eli the priest sat upon a seat by a post of the temple of the LORD.

And she was in bitterness of soul, and prayed unto the LORD, and wept sore.

And she vowed a vow, and said, O LORD of hosts, if thou wilt indeed look on the affliction of thine handmaid, and remember me, and not forget thine handmaid, but wilt give unto thine handmaid a man child, then I will give him unto the LORD all the days of his life, and there shall no razor come upon his head.

And it came to pass, as she continued praying before the LORD, that Eli marked her mouth.

Now Hannah, she spake in her heart; only her lips moved, but her voice was not heard: therefore Eli thought she had been drunken.

And Eli said unto her, How long wilt thou be drunken? put away thy wine from thee.

And Hannah answered and said, No, my lord, I am a woman of a sorrowful spirit: I have drunk neither wine nor strong drink, but have poured out my soul before the LORD.

Count not thine handmaid for a daughter of Belial: for out of the abundance of my complaint and grief have I spoken hitherto.

Then Eli answered and said, Go in peace: and the God of Israel grant thee thy petition that thou hast asked of him.

And she said, Let thine handmaid find grace in thy sight. So the woman went her way, and did eat, and her countenance was no more sad.

And they rose up in the morning early, and worshipped before the LORD, and returned, and came to their house to Ramah: and Elkanah knew Hannah his wife; and the LORD remembered her.

Wherefore it came to pass, when the time was come about after Hannah had conceived, that she bare a son, and called his name Samuel, saying, Because I have asked him of the LORD .

—1 Samuel 1:1–20

PRISCILLA

After these things Paul departed from Athens, and came to Corinth;

And found a certain Jew named Aquila, born in Pontus, lately come from Italy, with his wife Priscilla; (because that Claudius had commanded all Jews to depart from Rome:) and came unto them. . . .

And a certain Jew named Apollos, born at Alexandria, an eloquent man, and mighty in the scriptures, came to Ephesus.

This man was instructed in the way of the Lord; and being fervent in the spirit, he spake and taught diligently the things of the Lord, knowing only the baptism of John.

And he began to speak boldly in the synagogue: whom when Aquila and Priscilla had heard, they took him unto them, and expounded unto him the way of God more perfectly.

—Acts 18:1–2, 24–26

Lydia

And a certain woman named Lydia, a seller of purple, of the city of Thyatira, which worshipped God, heard us: whose heart the Lord opened, that she attended unto the things which were spoken of Paul.

And when she was baptized, and her household, she besought us, saying, If ye have judged me to be faithful to the Lord, come into my house, and abide there. And she constrained us.

—Acts 16:14–15

Wives of Strong Faith

Paul, an apostle of Jesus Christ by the will of God, according to the promise of life which is in Christ Jesus,

To Timothy, my dearly beloved son: Grace, mercy, and peace, from God the Father and Christ Jesus our Lord.

I thank God, whom I serve from my forefathers with pure conscience, that without ceasing I have remembrance of thee in my prayers night and day;

Greatly desiring to see thee, being mindful of thy tears, that I may be filled with joy;

When I call to remembrance the unfeigned faith that is in thee, which dwelt first in thy grandmother Lois, and thy mother Eunice; and I am persuaded that in thee also.

—2 Timothy 1:1–5

The Virtuous Woman

Who can find a virtuous woman? for her price is far above rubies.

The heart of her husband doth safely trust in her, so that he shall have no need of spoil.

She will do him good and not evil all the days of her life.

She seeketh wool, and flax, and worketh willingly with her hands.

She is like the merchants' ships; she bringeth her food from afar.

She riseth also while it is yet night, and giveth meat to her household, and a portion to her maidens.

She considereth a field, and buyeth it: with the fruit of her hands she planteth a vineyard.

She girdeth her loins with strength, and strengtheneth her arms.

She perceiveth that her merchandise is good: her candle goeth not out by night.

She layeth her hands to the spindle, and her hands hold the distaff.

She stretcheth out her hand to the poor; yea, she reacheth forth her hands to the needy.

She is not afraid of the snow for her household: for all her household are clothed with scarlet.

She maketh herself coverings of tapestry; her clothing is silk and purple.

Her husband is known in the gates, when he sitteth among the elders of the land.

She maketh fine linen, and selleth it; and delivereth girdles unto the merchant.

Strength and honour are her clothing; and she shall rejoice in time to come.

She openeth her mouth with wisdom; and in her tongue is the law of kindness.

She looketh well to the ways of her household, and eateth not the bread of idleness.

Her children arise up, and call her blessed; her husband also, and he praiseth her.

Many daughters have done virtuously, but thou excellest them all.

Favour is deceitful, and beauty is vain: but a woman that feareth the LORD, she shall be praised.

Give her of the fruit of her hands; and let her own works praise her in the gates.

—Proverbs 31:10–31

—Two—

So, You're Leaving Home!

What a jumbled mixture of feelings! Sure, you're happy to be launching into this brand new adventure of marriage. Then again, there were certain benefits to living in the family you're now leaving. Or have you been out on your own already for several years? Either way, the prospect of leaving behind what you now call "home" brings the latest chapter in your life to a close—and opens a new one.

Hard to Leave Parents Behind?

How many hopes and fears, how many ardent wishes and anxious apprehensions are twisted together in the threads that connect the parent with the child!

—Samuel Goodrich[1]

To every thing there is a season, and a time to every purpose under the heaven:

A time to be born, and a time to die; a time to plant, and a time to pluck up that which is planted;

A time to kill, and a time to heal; a time to break down, and a time to build up;

A time to weep, and a time to laugh; a time to mourn, and a time to dance;

A time to cast away stones, and a time to gather stones together; a time to embrace, and a time to refrain from embracing;

A time to get, and a time to lose; a time to keep, and a time to cast away;

A time to rend, and a time to sew; a time to keep silence, and a time to speak;

A time to love, and a time to hate; a time of war, and a time of peace.

—*Ecclesiastes 3:1–8*

Therefore shall a man leave his father and his mother, and shall cleave unto his wife: and they shall be one flesh.

—*Genesis 2:24*

❤ *Joyfully Celebrate Your New Situation*

The LORD is the portion of mine inheritance and of my cup: thou maintainest my lot.

The lines are fallen unto me in pleasant places; yea, I have a goodly heritage.

—*Psalm 16:5–6*

O come, let us sing unto the LORD: let us make a joyful noise to the rock of our salvation.

Let us come before his presence with thanksgiving, and make a joyful noise unto him with psalms.

For the LORD is a great God, and a great King above all gods.

In his hand are the deep places of the earth: the strength of the hills is his also.

The sea is his, and he made it: and his hands formed the dry land.

O come, let us worship and bow down: let us kneel before the LORD our maker.

For he is our God; and we are the people of his pasture, and the sheep of his hand.

—Psalm 95:1–7a

❤ *Find a Church Home, and Use Your Gifts*

Then they that gladly received his word were baptized: and the same day there were added unto them about three thousand souls.

And they continued stedfastly in the apostles' doctrine and fellowship, and in breaking of bread, and in prayers.

—Acts 2:41–42

If we say that we have fellowship with him, and walk in darkness, we lie, and do not the truth:

But if we walk in the light, as he is in the light, we have fellowship one with another, and the blood of Jesus Christ his Son cleanseth us from all sin.

—1 John 1:6–7

Now there are diversities of gifts, but the same Spirit.

And there are differences of administrations, but the same Lord.

And there are diversities of operations, but it is the same God which worketh all in all.

But the manifestation of the Spirit is given to every man to profit withal.

For to one is given by the Spirit the word of wisdom; to another the word of knowledge by the same Spirit;

To another faith by the same Spirit; to another the gifts of healing by the same Spirit;

To another the working of miracles; to another prophecy; to another discerning of spirits; to another divers kinds of tongues; to another the interpretation of tongues:

But all these worketh that one and the selfsame Spirit, dividing to every man severally as he will.

—1 Corinthians 12:4–11

But unto every one of us is given grace according to the measure of the gift of Christ. . . .

And he gave some, apostles; and some, prophets; and some, evangelists; and some, pastors and teachers;

For the perfecting of the saints, for the work of the ministry, for the edifying of the body of Christ:

Till we all come in the unity of the faith, and of the knowledge of the Son of God, unto a perfect man, unto the measure of the stature of the fulness of Christ:

That we henceforth be no more children, tossed to and fro, and carried about with every wind of doctrine, by the sleight of men, and cunning craftiness, whereby they lie in wait to deceive;

But speaking the truth in love, may grow up into him in all things, which is the head, even Christ:

From whom the whole body fitly joined together and compacted by that which every joint supplieth, according to the effectual working in the measure of every part, maketh increase of the body unto the edifying of itself in love.

—*Ephesians 4:7, 11–16*

And above all things have fervent charity among yourselves: for charity shall cover the multitude of sins.

—*1 Peter 4:8*

Even Married, You'll Still Have Lonely Times

Surprise, surprise . . . marriage does not make us immune to the same longings we struggled with as single people. We are ever tempted to find our security, self-esteem, and sexual satisfaction outside God's

prescribed boundaries. We can forsake one another in many ways—emotional and spiritual, as well as physical. The best protection is a lifelong goal of exploring to the depths the joy of our marriage bond and reconfirming our love and commitment often and earnestly.

—David LaPlaca[2]

Let us offer the sacrifice of praise to God continually, that is, the fruit of our lips giving thanks to his name.

—Hebrews 13:15

For thy Maker is thine husband; the LORD of hosts is his name; and thy Redeemer the Holy One of Israel; The God of the whole earth shall he be called.

For the LORD hath called thee as a woman forsaken and grieved in spirit, and a wife of youth, when thou wast refused, saith thy God.

For a small moment have I forsaken thee; but with great mercies will I gather thee.

In a little wrath I hid my face from thee for a moment; but with everlasting kindness will I have mercy on thee, saith the LORD thy Redeemer.

For this is as the waters of Noah unto me: for as I have sworn that the waters of Noah should no more go over the earth; so have I sworn that I would not be wroth with thee, nor rebuke thee.

For the mountains shall depart, and the hills be removed; but my kindness shall not depart from thee, neither shall the covenant of my peace be removed, saith the LORD that hath mercy on thee.

—Isaiah 54:5–10

For the LORD will not cast off his people, neither will he forsake his inheritance.

—Psalm 94:14

I the LORD have called thee in righteousness, and will hold thine hand, and will keep thee, and give thee for a covenant of the people, for a light of the Gentiles.

—Isaiah 42:6

So Build a Broad Network of Support

Marriage resembles a pair of shears, so joined that they cannot be separated; often moving in opposite directions, yet always punishing any one who comes between them.

—Sydney Smith[3]

Not forsaking the assembling of ourselves together, as the manner of some is; but exhorting one another: and so much the more, as ye see the day approaching.

—Hebrews 10:25

Wherefore comfort yourselves together, and edify one another, even as also ye do. . . .

Now we exhort you, brethren, warn them that are unruly, comfort the feebleminded, support the weak, be patient toward all men.

—1 Thessalonians 5:11, 14

There is one body, and one Spirit, even as ye are called in one hope of your calling;

One Lord, one faith, one baptism,

One God and Father of all, who is above all, and through all, and in you all.

—*Ephesians 4:4–6*

For as the body is one, and hath many members, and all the members of that one body, being many, are one body: so also is Christ.

For by one Spirit are we all baptized into one body, whether we be Jews or Gentiles, whether we be bond or free; and have been all made to drink into one Spirit.

For the body is not one member, but many.

If the foot shall say, Because I am not the hand, I am not of the body; is it therefore not of the body?

And if the ear shall say, Because I am not the eye, I am not of the body; is it therefore not of the body?

If the whole body were an eye, where were the hearing? If the whole were hearing, where were the smelling?

But now hath God set the members every one of them in the body, as it hath pleased him.

And if they were all one member, where were the body?

But now are they many members, yet but one body.

And the eye cannot say unto the hand, I have no need of thee: nor again the head to the feet, I have no need of you.

Nay, much more those members of the body, which seem to be more feeble, are necessary:

And those members of the body, which we think to be less honourable, upon these we bestow more abundant honour; and our uncomely parts have more abundant comeliness.

For our comely parts have no need: but God hath tempered the body together, having given more abundant honour to that part which lacked:

That there should be no schism in the body, but that the members should have the same care one for another.

And whether one member suffer, all the members suffer with it; or one member be honoured, all the members rejoice with it.

—1 Corinthians 12:12–26

Learn to Love Your In-Laws

Despite the fact that mother-in-law jokes still abound, the responsibility for making in-law relationships work belongs to all of us.

—Penny Bilofsky and Fredda Sacharow[4]

❤ *Moses and His Father-in-Law*

And it came to pass on the morrow, that Moses sat to judge the people: and the people stood by Moses from the morning unto the evening.

And when Moses' father in law saw all that he did to the people, he said, What is this thing that thou doest to the people? why sittest thou thyself alone, and all the people stand by thee from morning unto even?

And Moses said unto his father in law, Because the people come unto me to enquire of God:

When they have a matter, they come unto me; and I judge between one and another, and I do make them know the statutes of God, and his laws.

And Moses' father in law said unto him, The thing that thou doest is not good.

Thou wilt surely wear away, both thou, and this people that is with thee: for this thing is too heavy for thee: thou art not able to perform it thyself alone.

Hearken now unto my voice, I will give thee counsel, and God shall be with thee: Be thou for the people to God-ward, that thou mayest bring the causes unto God:

And thou shalt teach them ordinances and laws, and shalt shew them the way wherein they must walk, and the work that they must do.

Moreover thou shalt provide out of all the people able men, such as fear God, men of truth, hating covetousness; and place such over them, to be rulers of thousands, and rulers of hundreds, rulers of fifties, and rulers of tens:

And let them judge the people at all seasons: and it shall be, that every great matter they shall bring unto thee, but every small matter they shall judge: so shall it be easier for thyself, and they shall bear the burden with thee.

If thou shalt do this thing, and God command thee so, then thou shalt be able to endure, and all this people shall also go to their place in peace.

So Moses hearkened to the voice of his father in law, and did all that he had said.

—Exodus 18:13–24

❤ *Ruth and Her Mother-in-Law*

Now it came to pass in the days when the judges ruled, that there was a famine in the land. And a certain man of Bethlehem-judah went to sojourn in the country of Moab, he, and his wife, and his two sons.

And the name of the man was Elimelech, and the name of his wife Naomi, and the name of his two sons Mahlon and Chilion, Ephrathites of Bethlehem-judah. And they came into the country of Moab, and continued there.

And Elimelech Naomi's husband died; and she was left, and her two sons.

And they took them wives of the women of Moab; the name of the one was Orpah, and the name of the other Ruth: and they dwelled there about ten years.

And Mahlon and Chilion died also both of them; and the woman was left of her two sons and her husband. . . .

And Naomi said, Turn again, my daughters: why will ye go with me? are there yet any more sons in my womb, that they may be your husbands?

Turn again, my daughters, go your way; for I am too old to have an husband. If I should say, I have hope, if I should have an husband also tonight, and should also bear sons;

Would ye tarry for them till they were grown? would ye stay for them from having husbands? nay, my daughters; for it grieveth me much for your sakes that the hand of the LORD is gone out against me.

And they lifted up their voice, and wept again: and Orpah kissed her mother in law; but Ruth clave unto her.

And she said, Behold, thy sister in law is gone back unto her people, and unto her gods: return thou after thy sister in law.

And Ruth said, Intreat me not to leave thee, or to return from following after thee: for whither thou goest, I will go; and where thou lodgest, I will lodge: thy people shall be my people, and thy God my God:

Where thou diest, will I die, and there will I be buried: the LORD do so to me, and more also, if ought but death part thee and me. . . .

So Boaz took Ruth, and she was his wife: and when he went in unto her, the LORD gave her conception, and she bare a son.

And the women said unto Naomi, Blessed be the LORD, which hath not left thee this day without a kinsman, that his name may be famous in Israel.

And he shall be unto thee a restorer of thy life, and a nourisher of thine old age: for thy daughter in law, which loveth thee, which is better to thee than seven sons, hath borne him.

And Naomi took the child, and laid it in her bosom, and became nurse unto it.

—Ruth 1:1–5, 11–17; 4:13–16

—Three—

Build Your Home on the Lord

The wedding is over. The thank-you notes have been sent. The gifts have been placed on the shelf. Maybe you've even survived the first week or two without a significant quarrel of any kind! So, now it's late Saturday night. What are your plans for the morning?

Your Priority: Knowing and Serving the Lord

Source of all Life and Love, let this family be
a place of warmth on a cold night,
a friendly haven for the lonely stranger,
a small sanctuary of peace in the midst of
swirling activity.
Above all, let all its members seek to reflect
the kindness
of Your own heart, day by day.

—*Gary Wilde*[1]

And if it seem evil unto you to serve the LORD, choose you this day whom ye will serve; whether the gods which your fathers served that were on the other side of the flood, or the gods of the Amorites, in whose land ye dwell: but as for me and my house, we will serve the LORD.

—*Joshua 24:15*

Let the words of my mouth, and the meditation of my heart, be acceptable in thy sight, O LORD, my strength, and my redeemer.

—Psalm 19:14

Thy word have I hid in mine heart, that I might not sin against thee.

Blessed art thou, O LORD: teach me thy statutes.

With my lips have I declared all the judgments of thy mouth.

I have rejoiced in the way of thy testimonies, as much as in all riches.

I will meditate in thy precepts, and have respect unto thy ways.

I will delight myself in thy statutes: I will not forget thy word. . . .

Princes also did sit and speak against me: but thy servant did meditate in thy statutes. . . .

My hands also will I lift up unto thy commandments, which I have loved; and I will meditate in thy statutes. . . .

I have remembered thy name, O LORD, in the night, and have kept thy law. . . .

I thought on my ways, and turned my feet unto thy testimonies. . . .

O how love I thy law! it is my meditation all the day.

Thou through thy commandments hast made me wiser than mine enemies: for they are ever with me.

I have more understanding than all my teachers: for thy testimonies are my meditation.

—Psalm 119:11–16, 23, 48, 55, 59, 97–99

How precious also are thy thoughts unto me, O God! how great is the sum of them!

If I should count them, they are more in number than the sand: when I awake, I am still with thee.

—Psalm 139:17–18

❤ *Immerse Yourselves in His Word*

Thy word have I hid in mine heart, that I might not sin against thee. . . .

I will delight myself in thy statutes: I will not forget thy word. . . .

So shall I have wherewith to answer him that reproacheth me: for I trust in thy word. . . .

This is my comfort in my affliction: for thy word hath quickened me.

—Pslam 119:11, 16, 42, 50

Thy word is a lamp unto my feet, and a light unto my path.

I have sworn, and I will perform it, that I will keep thy righteous judgments.

I am afflicted very much: quicken me, O LORD, according unto thy word.

Accept, I beseech thee, the freewill offerings of my mouth, O LORD, and teach me thy judgments.

My soul is continually in my hand: yet do I not forget thy law.

The wicked have laid a snare for me: yet I erred not from thy precepts.

Thy testimonies have I taken as an heritage for ever: for they are the rejoicing of my heart.

I have inclined mine heart to perform thy statutes alway, even unto the end.

I hate vain thoughts: but thy law do I love.

Thou art my hiding place and my shield: I hope in thy word.

Depart from me, ye evildoers: for I will keep the commandments of my God.

Uphold me according unto thy word, that I may live: and let me not be ashamed of my hope.

—Psalm 119:105–115

But evil men and seducers shall wax worse and worse, deceiving, and being deceived.

But continue thou in the things which thou hast learned and hast been assured of, knowing of whom thou hast learned them;

And that from a child thou hast known the holy scriptures, which are able to make thee wise unto salvation through faith which is in Christ Jesus.

All scripture is given by inspiration of God, and is profitable for doctrine, for reproof, for correction, for instruction in righteousness:

That the man of God may be perfect, throughly furnished unto all good works.

—2 Timothy 3:13–17

For the word of God is quick, and powerful, and sharper than any twoedged sword, piercing even to the dividing asunder of soul and spirit, and of the joints and marrow, and is a discerner of the thoughts and intents of the heart.

Neither is there any creature that is not manifest in his sight: but all things are naked and opened unto the eyes of him with whom we have to do.

—Hebrews 4:12–13

❤ *Commit to Constant Obedience*

And now, Israel, what doth the LORD thy God require of thee, but to fear the LORD thy God, to walk in all his ways, and to love him, and to serve the LORD thy God with all thy heart and with all thy soul,

To keep the commandments of the LORD, and his statutes, which I command thee this day for thy good?

—Deuteronomy 10:12–13

Blessed are the undefiled in the way, who walk in the law of the LORD.

Blessed are they that keep his testimonies, and that seek him with the whole heart.

They also do no iniquity: they walk in his ways.

Thou hast commanded us to keep thy precepts diligently.

O that my ways were directed to keep thy statutes!

—Psalm 119:1–5

But if a man be just, and do that which is lawful and right,

And hath not eaten upon the mountains, neither hath lifted up his eyes to the idols of the house of Israel, neither hath defiled his neighbour's wife, neither hath come near to a menstruous woman,

And hath not oppressed any, but hath restored to the debtor his pledge, hath spoiled none by violence, hath given his bread to the hungry, and hath covered the naked with a garment;

He that hath not given forth upon usury, neither hath taken any increase, that hath withdrawn his hand from iniquity, hath executed true judgment between man and man,

Hath walked in my statutes, and hath kept my judgments, to deal truly; he is just, he shall surely live, saith the Lord GOD.

—Ezekiel 18:5–9

The night is far spent, the day is at hand: let us therefore cast off the works of darkness, and let us put on the armour of light.

Let us walk honestly, as in the day; not in rioting and drunkenness, not in chambering and wantonness, not in strife and envying.

But put ye on the Lord Jesus Christ, and make not provision for the flesh, to fulfil the lusts thereof.

—Romans 13:12–14

I, therefore, the prisoner of the Lord, beseech you that ye walk worthy of the vocation wherewith ye are called,

With all lowliness and meekness, with longsuffering, forbearing one another in love.

—Ephesians 4:1–2

If ye then be risen with Christ, seek those things which are above, where Christ sitteth on the right hand of God.

Set your affection on things above, not on things on the earth.

For ye are dead, and your life is hid with Christ in God.

When Christ, who is our life, shall appear, then shall ye also appear with him in glory.

Mortify therefore your members which are upon the earth; fornication, uncleanness, inordinate affection, evil concupiscence, and covetousness, which is idolatry:

For which things' sake the wrath of God cometh on the children of disobedience:

In the which ye also walked some time, when ye lived in them.

But now ye also put off all these; anger, wrath, malice, blasphemy, filthy communication out of your mouth.

Lie not one to another, seeing that ye have put off the old man with his deeds;

And have put on the new man, which is renewed in knowledge after the image of him that created him.

—*Colossians 3:1–10*

Having your conversation honest among the Gentiles: that, whereas they speak against you as evildoers, they may by your good works, which they shall behold, glorify God in the day of visitation.

Submit yourselves to every ordinance of man for the Lord's sake: whether it be to the king, as supreme;

Or unto governors, as unto them that are sent by him for the punishment of evildoers, and for the praise of them that do well.

For so is the will of God, that with well doing ye may put to silence the ignorance of foolish men.

—1 Peter 2:12–15

❤ *Pray Together Regularly*

When thou prayest, thou shalt not be as the hypocrites are: for they love to pray standing in the synagogues and in the corners of the streets, that they may be seen of men. Verily I say unto you, They have their reward.

But thou, when thou prayest, enter into thy closet, and when thou hast shut thy door, pray to thy Father which is in secret; and thy Father which seeth in secret shall reward thee openly.

But when ye pray, use not vain repetitions, as the heathen do: for they think that they shall be heard for their much speaking.

Be not ye therefore like unto them: for your Father knoweth what things ye have need of, before ye ask him.

After this manner therefore pray ye: Our Father which art in heaven, Hallowed be thy name.

Thy kingdom come. Thy will be done in earth, as it is in heaven.

Give us this day our daily bread.

And forgive us our debts, as we forgive our debtors.

And lead us not into temptation, but deliver us from evil: For thine is the kingdom, and the power, and the glory, for ever. Amen.

—Matthew 6:5–13

Verily I say unto you, Whatsoever ye shall bind on earth shall be bound in heaven: and whatsoever ye shall loose on earth shall be loosed in heaven.

—Matthew 18:18

For we are saved by hope: but hope that is seen is not hope: for what a man seeth, why doth he yet hope for?

But if we hope for that we see not, then do we with patience wait for it.

Likewise the Spirit also helpeth our infirmities: for we know not what we should pray for as we ought: but the Spirit itself maketh intercession for us with groanings which cannot be uttered.

And he that searcheth the hearts knoweth what is the mind of the Spirit, because he maketh intercession for the saints according to the will of God.

And we know that all things work together for good to them that love God, to them who are the called according to his purpose.

—*Romans 8:24–28*

Let us therefore come boldly unto the throne of grace, that we may obtain mercy, and find grace to help in time of need.

—*Hebrews 4:16*

Let us draw near with a true heart in full assurance of faith, having our hearts sprinkled from an evil conscience, and our bodies washed with pure water.

—*Hebrews 10:22*

Is any among you afflicted? let him pray. Is any merry? let him sing psalms.

Is any sick among you? let him call for the elders of the church; and let them pray over him, anointing him with oil in the name of the Lord:

And the prayer of faith shall save the sick, and the Lord shall raise him up; and if he hath committed sins, they shall be forgiven him.

Confess your faults one to another, and pray one for another, that ye may be healed. The effectual fervent prayer of a righteous man availeth much.

Elias was a man subject to like passions as we are, and he prayed earnestly that it might not rain: and it rained not on the earth by the space of three years and six months.

And he prayed again, and the heaven gave rain, and the earth brought forth her fruit.

—James 5:13–18

And whatsoever we ask, we receive of him, because we keep his commandments, and do those things that are pleasing in his sight.

—1 John 3:22

These things have I written unto you that believe on the name of the Son of God; that ye may know that ye have eternal life, and that ye may believe on the name of the Son of God.

And this is the confidence that we have in him, that, if we ask any thing according to his will, he heareth us:

And if we know that he hear us, whatsoever we ask, we know that we have the petitions that we desired of him.

—*1 John 5:13–15*

Pray without ceasing.

—*1 Thessalonians 5:17*

❤ *Open Your Home and Hearts to Share Christ's Love*

No person, when he hath lighted a candle, covereth it with a vessel, or putteth it under a bed; but setteth it on a candlestick, that they which enter in may see the light. . . .

Now the man out of whom the devils were departed besought him that he might be with him: but Jesus sent him away, saying,

Return to thine own house, and shew how great things God hath done unto thee. And he went his way, and published throughout the whole city how great things Jesus had done unto him.

—Luke 8:16, 38–39

But whoso hath this world's good, and seeth his brother have need, and shutteth up his bowels of compassion from him, how dwelleth the love of God in him?

My little children, let us not love in word, neither in tongue; but in deed and in truth.

And hereby we know that we are of the truth, and shall assure our hearts before him.

—1 John 3:17–19

Whosoever shall confess me before men, him shall the Son of man also confess before the angels of God:

But he that denieth me before men shall be denied before the angels of God.

—Luke 12:8–9

For I am not ashamed of the gospel of Christ: for it is the power of God unto salvation to every one that believeth; to the Jew first, and also to the Greek.

For therein is the righteousness of God revealed from faith to faith: as it is written, The just shall live by faith.

—Romans 1:16–17

But sanctify the Lord God in your hearts: and be ready always to give an answer to every man that asketh you a reason of the hope that is in you with meekness and fear.

—1 Peter 3:15

Keep Growing In Faith

Marriage is our last, best chance to grow up.

—Joseph Barth

Not as though I had already attained, either were already perfect: but I follow after, if that I may apprehend that for which also I am apprehended of Christ Jesus.

Brethren, I count not myself to have apprehended: but this one thing I do, forgetting those things which are behind, and reaching forth unto those things which are before,

I press toward the mark for the prize of the high calling of God in Christ Jesus.

Let us therefore, as many as be perfect, be thus minded: and if in any thing ye be otherwise minded, God shall reveal even this unto you.

Nevertheless, whereto we have already attained, let us walk by the same rule, let us mind the same thing.

—Philippians 3:12–16

Now faith is the substance of things hoped for, the evidence of things not seen.

For by it the elders obtained a good report.

Through faith we understand that the worlds were framed by the word of God, so that things which are seen were not made of things which do appear.

By faith Abel offered unto God a more excellent sacrifice than Cain, by which he obtained witness that he was righteous, God testifying of his gifts: and by it he being dead yet speaketh.

By faith Enoch was translated that he should not see death; and was not found, because God had translated him: for before his translation he had this testimony, that he pleased God.

But without faith it is impossible to please him: for he that cometh to God must believe that he is, and that he is a rewarder of them that diligently seek him.

By faith Noah, being warned of God of things not seen as yet, moved with fear, prepared an ark to the saving of his house; by the which he condemned the world, and became heir of the righteousness which is by faith.

By faith Abraham, when he was called to go out into a place which he should after receive for an inheritance, obeyed; and he went out, not knowing whither he went.

By faith he sojourned in the land of promise, as in a strange country, dwelling in tabernacles with Isaac and Jacob, the heirs with him of the same promise:

For he looked for a city which hath foundations, whose builder and maker is God.

Through faith also Sarah herself received strength to conceive seed, and was delivered of a child when she was past age, because she judged him faithful who had promised.

Therefore sprang there even of one, and him as good as dead, so many as the stars of the sky in multitude, and as the sand which is by the sea shore innumerable.

These all died in faith, not having received the promises, but having seen them afar off, and were persuaded of them, and embraced them, and confessed that they were strangers and pilgrims on the earth.

For they that say such things declare plainly that they seek a country.

—*Hebrews 11:1–14*

For whatsoever is born of God overcometh the world: and this is the victory that overcometh the world, even our faith.

Who is he that overcometh the world, but he that believeth that Jesus is the Son of God?

—1 John 5:4–5

Verily I say unto you, If ye have faith as a grain of mustard seed, ye shall say unto this mountain, Remove hence to yonder place; and it shall remove; and nothing shall be impossible unto you.

—Matthew 17:20b

—Four—

How Will You Handle Your Conflicts?

You're not the only couple in the world to lock horns in a heated argument. But these true tests of your marriage will reveal your ability to work out ways to move ahead—again, and again, down through the years.

Yes, Conflict Will Come

If I see conflict as natural, neutral, normal, I may be able to see the difficulties we experience as tension in relationships and honest differences in perspective that can be worked through by caring about each other and confronting each other with truth expressed by love.

—*David Augsburger*[1]

And Adam knew Eve his wife; and she conceived, and bare Cain, and said, I have gotten a man from the LORD.

And she again bare his brother Abel. And Abel was a keeper of sheep, but Cain was a tiller of the ground.

And in process of time it came to pass, that Cain brought of the fruit of the ground an offering unto the LORD.

And Abel, he also brought of the firstlings of his flock and of the fat thereof. And the LORD had respect unto Abel and to his offering:

But unto Cain and to his offering he had not respect. And Cain was very wroth, and his countenance fell.

And the LORD said unto Cain, Why art thou wroth? and why is thy countenance fallen?

If thou doest well, shalt thou not be accepted? and if thou doest not well, sin lieth at the door. And unto thee shall be his desire, and thou shalt rule over him.

And Cain talked with Abel his brother: and it came to pass, when they were in the field, that Cain rose up against Abel his brother, and slew him.

—Genesis 4:1–8

And Lot also, which went with Abram, had flocks, and herds, and tents.

And the land was not able to bear them, that they might dwell together: for their substance was great, so that they could not dwell together.

And there was a strife between the herdmen of Abram's cattle and the herdmen of Lot's cattle: and the Canaanite and the Perizzite dwelled then in the land.

And Abram said unto Lot, Let there be no strife, I pray thee, between me and thee, and between my herdmen and thy herdmen; for we be brethren.

Is not the whole land before thee? separate thyself, I pray thee, from me: if thou wilt take the left hand, then I will go to the right; or if thou depart to the right hand, then I will go to the left.

And Lot lifted up his eyes, and beheld all the plain of Jordan, that it was well watered every where, before the LORD destroyed Sodom and Gomorrah, even as the garden of the LORD, like the land of Egypt, as thou comest unto Zoar.

Then Lot chose him all the plain of Jordan; and Lot journeyed east: and they separated themselves the one from the other.

Abram dwelled in the land of Canaan, and Lot dwelled in the cities of the plain, and pitched his tent toward Sodom.

—Genesis 13:5–12

Now his elder son was in the field: and as he came and drew nigh to the house, he heard musick and dancing.

And he called one of the servants, and asked what these things meant.

And he said unto him, Thy brother is come; and thy father hath killed the fatted calf, because he hath received him safe and sound.

And he was angry, and would not go in: therefore came his father out, and intreated him.

And he answering said to his father, Lo, these many years do I serve thee, neither transgressed I at any time thy commandment: and yet thou never gavest me a kid, that I might make merry with my friends:

But as soon as this thy son was come, which hath devoured thy living with harlots, thou hast killed for him the fatted calf.

And he said unto him, Son, thou art ever with me, and all that I have is thine.

It was meet that we should make merry, and be glad: for this thy brother was dead, and is alive again; and was lost, and is found.

—Luke 15:25–32

Think not that I am come to send peace on earth: I came not to send peace, but a sword.

For I am come to set a man at variance against his father, and the daughter against her mother, and the daughter in law against her mother in law.

And a man's foes shall be they of his own household.

He that loveth father or mother more than me is not worthy of me: and he that loveth son or daughter more than me is not worthy of me.

And he that taketh not his cross, and followeth after me, is not worthy of me.

He that findeth his life shall lose it: and he that loseth his life for my sake shall find it.

—Matthew 10:34–39

Again, think ye that we excuse ourselves unto you? we speak before God in Christ:

but we do all things, dearly beloved, for your edifying.

For I fear, lest, when I come, I shall not find you such as I would, and that I shall be found unto you such as ye would not: lest there be debates, envyings, wraths, strifes, backbitings, whisperings, swellings, tumults.

—2 Corinthians 12:19–20

Finally, be ye all of one mind, having compassion one of another, love as brethren, be pitiful, be courteous.

—1 Peter 3:8

❤ *Really Listen to One Another*

The heart of the prudent getteth knowledge; and the ear of the wise seeketh knowledge.

—Proverbs 18:15

Wherefore, Job, I pray thee, hear my speeches, and hearken to all my words.

Behold, now I have opened my mouth, my tongue hath spoken in my mouth.

My words shall be of the uprightness of my heart: and my lips shall utter knowledge clearly.

The Spirit of God hath made me, and the breath of the Almighty hath given me life.

If thou canst answer me, set thy words in order before me, stand up.

—Job 33:1–5

Then Samuel said unto Saul, Stay, and I will tell thee what the LORD hath said to me this night. And he said unto him, Say on.

—1 Samuel 15:16

A man hath joy by the answer of his mouth: and a word spoken in due season, how good is it!

—Proverbs 15:23

A word fitly spoken is like apples of gold in pictures of silver.

—Proverbs 25:11

❤ *Handle Your Anger Appropriately*

But I say unto you, That whosoever is angry with his brother without a cause shall be in danger of the judgment: and whosoever shall say to his brother, Raca, shall be in danger of the council: but whosoever shall say, Thou fool, shall be in danger of hell fire.

—Matthew 5:22

I will lift up mine eyes unto the hills, from whence cometh my help.

My help cometh from the LORD, which made heaven and earth.

He will not suffer thy foot to be moved: he that keepeth thee will not slumber.

Behold, he that keepeth Israel shall neither slumber nor sleep.

The LORD is thy keeper: the LORD is thy shade upon thy right hand.

The sun shall not smite thee by day, nor the moon by night.

The LORD shall preserve thee from all evil: he shall preserve thy soul.

The LORD shall preserve thy going out and thy coming in from this time forth, and even for evermore.

—Psalm 121:1–8

A soft answer turneth away wrath: but grievous words stir up anger.

The tongue of the wise useth knowledge aright: but the mouth of fools poureth out foolishness.

—Proverbs 15:1–2

Be ye angry, and sin not: let not the sun go down upon your wrath.

—Ephesians 4:26

❤ *Approach One Another with Humility*

The fear of the LORD is the instruction of wisdom; and before honour is humility.

—Proverbs 15:33

By humility and the fear of the LORD are riches, and honour, and life.

—Proverbs 22:4

But I say unto you, That ye resist not evil: but whosoever shall smite thee on thy right cheek, turn to him the other also.

—Matthew 5:39

For whosoever exalteth himself shall be abased; and he that humbleth himself shall be exalted.

—Luke 14:11

Do ye think that the scripture saith in vain, The spirit that dwelleth in us lusteth to envy?

But he giveth more grace. Wherefore he saith, God resisteth the proud, but giveth grace unto the humble.

—James 4:5–6

And he spake this parable unto certain which trusted in themselves that they were righteous, and despised others:

Two men went up into the temple to pray; the one a Pharisee, and the other a publican.

The Pharisee stood and prayed thus with himself, God, I thank thee, that I am not as other men are, extortioners, unjust, adulterers, or even as this publican.

I fast twice in the week, I give tithes of all that I possess.

And the publican, standing afar off, would not lift up so much as his eyes unto heaven, but smote upon his breast, saying, God be merciful to me a sinner.

I tell you, this man went down to his house justified rather than the other: for every one that exalteth himself shall be abased; and he that humbleth himself shall be exalted.

—Luke 18:9–14

Humble yourselves therefore under the mighty hand of God, that he may exalt you in due time.

—1 Peter 5:6

Keep Your Head, Keep Your Commitment

Bless us, Lord, as we weather this family conflict. We all have certain needs to be met, certain ways of trying to fulfill our dreams. Yet each of us seeks this one basic thing in the midst of it all: Love. Simply love.

—Gary Wilde[2]

Godliness with contentment is great gain.

For we brought nothing into this world, and it is certain we can carry nothing out.

And having food and raiment let us be therewith content.

—1 Timothy 6:6–8

Not that I speak in respect of want: for I have learned, in whatsoever state I am, therewith to be content.

I know both how to be abased, and I know how to abound: every where and in all things I am instructed both to be full and to be hungry, both to abound and to suffer need.

I can do all things through Christ which strengtheneth me.

—Philippians 4:11–13

Let your conversation be without covetousness; and be content with such things as ye have: for he hath said, I will never leave thee, nor forsake thee.

—Hebrews 13:5

Speak Kindly—But Directly

The genius of communication is the ability to be both totally honest and totally kind at the same time.

—John Powell[3]

But when Peter was come to Antioch, I withstood him to the face, because he was to be blamed.

For before that certain came from James, he did eat with the Gentiles: but when they were come, he withdrew and separated himself, fearing them which were of the circumcision.

And the other Jews dissembled likewise with him; insomuch that Barnabas also was carried away with their dissimulation.

But when I saw that they walked not uprightly according to the truth of the gospel, I said unto Peter before them all, If thou, being a Jew, livest after the manner of Gentiles, and not as do the Jews, why compellest thou the Gentiles to live as do the Jews?

We who are Jews by nature, and not sinners of the Gentiles,

Knowing that a man is not justified by the works of the law, but by the faith of Jesus Christ, even we have believed in Jesus Christ, that we might be justified by the faith of Christ, and not by the works of the law: for by the works of the law shall no flesh be justified.

—*Galatians 2:11–16*

But speaking the truth in love, may [you] grow up into him in all things, which is the head, even Christ:

From whom the whole body fitly joined together and compacted by that which every joint supplieth, according to the effectual working in the measure of every part, maketh increase of the body unto the edifying of itself in love.

—Ephesians 4:15–16

Speaking to yourselves in psalms and hymns and spiritual songs, singing and making melody in your heart to the Lord;

Giving thanks always for all things unto God and the Father in the name of our Lord Jesus Christ.

—Ephesians 5:19–20

But we were gentle among you, even as a nurse cherisheth her children.

—1 Thessalonians 2:7

Maintain a Spirit of Togetherness and Teamwork

Marriage is like a three-speed gearbox: affection, friendship, love. It is not advisable to crash your gears and go right through to love straightaway. You need to ease your way through. The basis of love is respect, and that needs to be learned from affection and friendship.

—Peter Ustinov[4]

And the LORD God planted a garden eastward in Eden; and there he put the man whom he had formed.

And out of the ground made the LORD God to grow every tree that is pleasant to the sight, and good for food; the tree of life also in the midst of the garden, and the tree of knowledge of good and evil.

And a river went out of Eden to water the garden; and from thence it was parted, and became into four heads.

The name of the first is Pison: that is it which compasseth the whole land of Havilah, where there is gold;

And the gold of that land is good: there is bdellium and the onyx stone.

And the name of the second river is Gihon: the same is it that compasseth the whole land of Ethiopia.

And the name of the third river is Hiddekel: that is it which goeth toward the east of Assyria. And the fourth river is Euphrates.

And the LORD God took the man, and put him into the garden of Eden to dress it and to keep it.

And the LORD God commanded the man, saying, Of every tree of the garden thou mayest freely eat:

But of the tree of the knowledge of good and evil, thou shalt not eat of it: for in the day that thou eatest thereof thou shalt surely die.

And the LORD God said, It is not good that the man should be alone; I will make him an help meet for him.

And out of the ground the LORD God formed every beast of the field, and every fowl of the air; and brought them unto Adam to see what he would call them: and whatsoever Adam called every living creature, that was the name thereof.

And Adam gave names to all cattle, and to the fowl of the air, and to every beast of the field; but for Adam there was not found an help meet for him.

And the LORD God caused a deep sleep to fall upon Adam, and he slept: and he took one of his ribs, and closed up the flesh instead thereof;

And the rib, which the LORD God had taken from man, made he a woman, and brought her unto the man.

And Adam said, This is now bone of my bones, and flesh of my flesh: she shall be called Woman, because she was taken out of Man.

Therefore shall a man leave his father and his mother, and shall cleave unto his wife: and they shall be one flesh.

And they were both naked, the man and his wife, and were not ashamed.

—Genesis 2:8–25

Two are better than one; because they have a good reward for their labour.

For if they fall, the one will lift up his fellow: but woe to him that is alone when he falleth; for he hath not another to help him up.

Again, if two lie together, then they have heat: but how can one be warm alone?

And if one prevail against him, two shall withstand him; and a threefold cord is not quickly broken.

—*Ecclesiastes 4:9–12*

Remind One Another of God's Blessings

I would maintain that thanks are the highest form of thought; and that gratitude is happiness doubled by wonder.

—*G. K. Chesterton*[5]

Blessed be the God and Father of our Lord Jesus Christ, who hath blessed us with all spiritual blessings in heavenly places in Christ:

According as he hath chosen us in him before the foundation of the world, that we should be holy and without blame before him in love:

Having predestinated us unto the adoption of children by Jesus Christ to himself, according to the good pleasure of his will,

To the praise of the glory of his grace, wherein he hath made us accepted in the beloved.

In whom we have redemption through his blood, the forgiveness of sins, according to the riches of his grace;

Wherein he hath abounded toward us in all wisdom and prudence;

Having made known unto us the mystery of his will, according to his good pleasure which he hath purposed in himself:

That in the dispensation of the fulness of times he might gather together in one all things in Christ, both which are in heaven, and which are on earth; even in him:

In whom also we have obtained an inheritance, being predestinated according to the purpose of him who worketh all things after the counsel of his own will:

That we should be to the praise of his glory, who first trusted in Christ.

In whom ye also trusted, after that ye heard the word of truth, the gospel of your salvation: in whom also after that ye believed, ye were sealed with that holy Spirit of promise,

Which is the earnest of our inheritance until the redemption of the purchased possession, unto the praise of his glory.

—*Ephesians 1:3–14*

For this cause we also, since the day we heard it, do not cease to pray for you, and to desire that ye might be filled with the knowledge of his will in all wisdom and spiritual understanding;

That ye might walk worthy of the Lord unto all pleasing, being fruitful in every good work, and increasing in the knowledge of God;

Strengthened with all might, according to his glorious power, unto all patience and longsuffering with joyfulness;

Giving thanks unto the Father, which hath made us meet to be partakers of the inheritance of the saints in light.

—Colossians 1:9–12

Every good gift and every perfect gift is from above, and cometh down from the Father of lights, with whom is no variableness, neither shadow of turning.

Of his own will begat he us with the word of truth, that we should be a kind of firstfruits of his creatures.

—James 1:17–18

He turneth the wilderness into a standing water, and dry ground into watersprings.

And there he maketh the hungry to dwell, that they may prepare a city for habitation;

And sow the fields, and plant vineyards, which may yield fruits of increase.

He blesseth them also, so that they are multiplied greatly; and suffereth not their cattle to decrease.

—Psalm 107:35–38

—Five—

Can You Pull Together in the Tough Times?

Adversity has a way of driving a wedge between couples, of making you say things you wish you hadn't, passing blame when you should be pulling together. That's when love becomes a deliberate decision, when forgiveness and support take precedence over gut reactions and selfish demands.

When Adversity Strikes

A teenage girl was examining her grandmother's wedding ring. The girl said, "Wow, what heavy and cumbersome rings those were fifty years ago." The grandmother replied, "That's true, but don't forget that in my day they were made to last a lifetime."

—Anonymous[1]

My brethren, count it all joy when ye fall into divers temptations;

Knowing this, that the trying of your faith worketh patience.

But let patience have her perfect work, that ye may be perfect and entire, wanting nothing.

—James 1:2–4

Woe unto him that striveth with his Maker! Let the potsherd strive with the potsherds of the earth. Shall the clay say to him that fashioneth it, What makest thou? or thy work, He hath no hands?

—Isaiah 45:9

Thou therefore endure hardness, as a good soldier of Jesus Christ.

No man that warreth entangleth himself with the affairs of this life; that he may please him who hath chosen him to be a soldier.

And if a man also strive for masteries, yet is he not crowned, except he strive lawfully.

—2 Timothy 2:3–5

Rejoicing in hope; patient in tribulation; continuing instant in prayer.

—Romans 12:12

So that we ourselves glory in you in the churches of God for your patience and faith in all your persecutions and tribulations that ye endure:

Which is a manifest token of the righteous judgment of God, that ye may be counted worthy of the kingdom of God, for which ye also suffer.

—2 Thessalonians 1:4–5

In Times of Trouble

God give burdens, also shoulders.

—*Yiddish proverb*

He shall deliver thee in six troubles: yea, in seven there shall no evil touch thee.

—*Job 5:19*

I waited patiently for the LORD; and he inclined unto me, and heard my cry.

He brought me up also out of an horrible pit, out of the miry clay, and set my feet upon a rock, and established my goings.

And he hath put a new song in my mouth, even praise unto our God: many shall see it, and fear, and shall trust in the LORD.

Blessed is that man that maketh the LORD his trust.

—*Psalm 40:1–4a*

And we know that all things work together for good to them that love God, to them who are the called according to his purpose.

—Romans 8:28

We are troubled on every side, yet not distressed; we are perplexed, but not in despair;

Persecuted, but not forsaken; cast down, but not destroyed.

—2 Corinthians 4:8–9

Wherein ye greatly rejoice, though now for a season, if need be, ye are in heaviness through manifold temptations:

That the trial of your faith, being much more precious than of gold that perisheth, though it be tried with fire, might be found unto praise and honour and glory at the appearing of Jesus Christ.

—1 Peter 1:6–7

❤ *Go to God in Prayer—Together*

Seeing then that we have a great high priest, that is passed into the heavens, Jesus the Son of God, let us hold fast our profession.

For we have not an high priest which cannot be touched with the feeling of our infirmities; but was in all points tempted like as we are, yet without sin.

Let us therefore come boldly unto the throne of grace, that we may obtain mercy, and find grace to help in time of need.

—Hebrews 4:14–16

And he spake a parable unto them to this end, that men ought always to pray, and not to faint;

Saying, There was in a city a judge, which feared not God, neither regarded man:

And there was a widow in that city; and she came unto him, saying, Avenge me of mine adversary.

And he would not for a while: but afterward he said within himself, Though I fear not God, nor regard man;

Yet because this widow troubleth me, I will avenge her, lest by her continual coming she weary me.

And the Lord said, Hear what the unjust judge saith.

And shall not God avenge his own elect, which cry day and night unto him, though he bear long with them?

I tell you that he will avenge them speedily. Nevertheless when the Son of man cometh, shall he find faith on the earth?

—Luke 18:1–8

Behold, the eye of the LORD is upon them that fear him, upon them that hope in his mercy;

To deliver their soul from death, and to keep them alive in famine.

—Psalm 33:18–19

I will also save you from all your uncleannesses: and I will call for the corn, and will increase it, and lay no famine upon you.

And I will multiply the fruit of the tree, and the increase of the field, that ye shall receive no more reproach of famine among the heathen.

—Ezekiel 36:29–30

The LORD is my shepherd; I shall not want.

He maketh me to lie down in green pastures: he leadeth me beside the still waters.

He restoreth my soul: he leadeth me in the paths of righteousness for his name's sake.

Yea, though I walk through the valley of the shadow of death, I will fear no evil: for thou art with me; thy rod and thy staff they comfort me.

—Psalm 23:1–4

And such trust have we through Christ to God-ward:

Not that we are sufficient of ourselves to think any thing as of ourselves; but our sufficiency is of God.

—2 Corinthians 3:4–5

❤ *God Is With You in This*

Verily I have cleansed my heart in vain, and washed my hands in innocency.

For all the day long have I been plagued, and chastened every morning.

If I say, I will speak thus; behold, I should offend against the generation of thy children.

When I thought to know this, it was too painful for me;

Until I went into the sanctuary of God; then understood I their end.

—Psalm 73:13–17

Fear thou not; for I am with thee: be not dismayed; for I am thy God: I will strengthen thee; yea, I will help thee; yea, I will uphold thee with the right hand of my righteousness.

—Isaiah 41:10

Peace I leave with you, my peace I give unto you: not as the world giveth, give I unto you. Let not your heart be troubled, neither let it be afraid.

—John 14:27

Come unto me, all ye that labour and are heavy laden, and I will give you rest.

Take my yoke upon you, and learn of me; for I am meek and lowly in heart: and ye shall find rest unto your souls.

For my yoke is easy, and my burden is light.

—Matthew 11:28–30

If the Son therefore shall make you free, ye shall be free indeed.

—John 8:36

Are the Stresses of Life Overwhelming You?

In order to realize the worth of the anchor, we need to feel the stress of the storm.

—Anonymous

Now there arose up a new king over Egypt, which knew not Joseph.

And he said unto his people, Behold, the people of the children of Israel are more and mightier than we:

Come on, let us deal wisely with them; lest they multiply, and it come to pass, that, when there falleth out any war, they join also unto our enemies, and fight against us, and so get them up out of the land.

Therefore they did set over them taskmasters to afflict them with their burdens. And they built for Pharaoh treasure cities, Pithom and Raamses.

But the more they afflicted them, the more they multiplied and grew. And they were grieved because of the children of Israel.

And the Egyptians made the children of Israel to serve with rigour:

And they made their lives bitter with hard bondage, in morter, and in brick, and in all manner of service in the field: all their service, wherein they made them serve, was with rigour.

—Exodus 1:8–14

Now it came to pass, as they went, that he entered into a certain village: and a certain woman named Martha received him into her house.

And she had a sister called Mary, which also sat at Jesus' feet, and heard his word.

But Martha was cumbered about much serving, and came to him, and said, Lord, dost thou not care that my sister hath left me to serve alone? bid her therefore that she help me.

And Jesus answered and said unto her, Martha, Martha, thou art careful and troubled about many things:

But one thing is needful: and Mary hath chosen that good part, which shall not be taken away from her.

—Luke 10:38–42

But what things were gain to me, those I counted loss for Christ.

Yea doubtless, and I count all things but loss for the excellency of the knowledge of Christ Jesus my Lord: for whom I have suffered the loss of all things, and do count them but dung, that I may win Christ,

And be found in him, not having mine own righteousness, which is of the law, but that which is through the faith of Christ, the righteousness which is of God by faith:

That I may know him, and the power of his resurrection, and the fellowship of his sufferings, being made conformable unto his death;

If by any means I might attain unto the resurrection of the dead.

—Philippians 3:7–11

Be not thou therefore ashamed of the testimony of our Lord, nor of me his prisoner: but be thou partaker of the afflictions of the gospel according to the power of God;

Who hath saved us, and called us with an holy calling, not according to our works, but according to his own purpose and grace, which was given us in Christ Jesus before the world began.

—2 Timothy 1:8–9

❤ *God's Strength Is Your Salvation*

Hear, O Israel: Thou art to pass over Jordan this day, to go in to possess nations greater and mightier than thyself, cities great and fenced up to heaven,

A people great and tall, the children of the Anakims, whom thou knowest, and of whom thou hast heard say, Who can stand before the children of Anak!

Understand therefore this day, that the LORD thy God is he which goeth over before thee; as a consuming fire he shall destroy them, and he shall bring them down before thy face: so shalt thou drive them out, and destroy them quickly, as the LORD hath said unto thee.

—Deuteronomy 9:1–3

We have heard with our ears, O God, our fathers have told us, what work thou didst in their days, in the times of old.

How thou didst drive out the heathen with thy hand, and plantedst them; how thou didst afflict the people, and cast them out.

For they got not the land in possession by their own sword, neither did their own arm save them: but thy right hand, and thine arm, and the light of thy countenance, because thou hadst a favour unto them.

—Psalm 44:1–3

God is our refuge and strength, a very present help in trouble.

Therefore will not we fear, though the earth be removed, and though the mountains be carried into the midst of the sea;

Though the waters thereof roar and be troubled, though the mountains shake with the swelling thereof.

—*Psalm 46:1–3*

Blessed is the man whose strength is in thee; in whose heart are the ways of them.

Who passing through the valley of Baca make it a well; the rain also filleth the pools.

They go from strength to strength, every one of them in Zion appeareth before God.

—*Psalm 84:5–7*

Blessed are ye, when men shall revile you, and persecute you, and shall say all manner of evil against you falsely, for my sake.

Rejoice, and be exceeding glad for great is your reward in heaven: for so persecuted they the prophets which were before you.

—*Matthew 5:11–12*

For in the time of trouble he shall hide me in his pavilion: in the secret of his tabernacle shall he hide me; he shall set me up upon a rock.

—Psalm 27:5

No weapon that is formed against thee shall prosper; and every tongue that shall rise against thee in judgment thou shalt condemn. This is the heritage of the servants of the LORD, and their righteousness is of me, saith the LORD.

—Isaiah 54:17

So shall they fear the name of the LORD from the west, and his glory from the rising of the sun. When the enemy shall come in like a flood, the Spirit of the LORD shall lift up a standard against him.

—Isaiah 59:19

❤ *Remember: You Are God's Beloved Creation!*

God created man in his own image, in the image of God created he him; male and female created he them.

And God blessed them, and God said unto them, Be fruitful, and multiply, and replenish the earth, and subdue it: and have dominion over the fish of the sea, and over the fowl of the air, and over every living thing that moveth upon the earth.

And God said, Behold, I have given you every herb bearing seed, which is upon the face of all the earth, and every tree, in the which is the fruit of a tree yielding seed; to you it shall be for meat.

And to every beast of the earth, and to every fowl of the air, and to every thing that creepeth upon the earth, wherein there is life, I have given every green herb for meat: and it was so.

And God saw every thing that he had made, and, behold, it was very good. And the evening and the morning were the sixth day.

—Genesis 1:27–31

I will praise thee; for I am fearfully and wonderfully made: marvellous are thy works; and that my soul knoweth right well.

My substance was not hid from thee, when I was made in secret, and curiously wrought in the lowest parts of the earth.

Thine eyes did see my substance, yet being unperfect; and in thy book all my members were written, which in continuance were fashioned, when as yet there was none of them.

—Psalm 139:14–16

O LORD our Lord, how excellent is thy name in all the earth! who hast set thy glory above the heavens.

Out of the mouth of babes and sucklings hast thou ordained strength because of thine enemies, that thou mightest still the enemy and the avenger.

When I consider thy heavens, the work of thy fingers, the moon and the stars, which thou hast ordained;

What is man, that thou art mindful of him? and the son of man, that thou visitest him?

For thou hast made him a little lower than the angels, and hast crowned him with glory and honour.

Thou madest him to have dominion over the works of thy hands; thou hast put all things under his feet:

All sheep and oxen, yea, and the beasts of the field;

The fowl of the air, and the fish of the sea, and whatsoever passeth through the paths of the seas.

O LORD our Lord, how excellent is thy name in all the earth!

—*Psalm 8:1–9*

For we are his workmanship, created in Christ Jesus unto good works, which God hath before ordained that we should walk in them.

—*Ephesians 2:10*

So Let God Comfort You in All Circumstances

There is a place of quiet rest,
Near to the heart of God.

—Christian hymn

In the multitude of my thoughts within me thy comforts delight my soul.

—Psalm 94:19

For he maketh sore, and bindeth up: he woundeth, and his hands make whole.

—Job 5:18

Praise ye the LORD: for it is good to sing praises unto our God; for it is pleasant; and praise is comely.

The LORD doth build up Jerusalem: he gathereth together the outcasts of Israel.

He healeth the broken in heart, and bindeth up their wounds.

—Psalm 147:1–3

Therefore all they that devour thee shall be devoured; and all thine adversaries, every one of them, shall go into captivity; and they that spoil thee shall be a spoil, and all that prey upon thee will I give for a prey.

For I will restore health unto thee, and I will heal thee of thy wounds, saith the LORD; because they called thee an Outcast, saying, This is Zion, whom no man seeketh after.

—Jeremiah 30:16–17

—Six—

Keep the Romance Alive

"I love you, but . . ." Those three beautiful words! But . . . but. That one small conjunction ruins everything. We humans want to add conditions to our love, probably because we know at some deep level that the essence of love is self-sacrifice. The deeper the love, the more complete the quality of self-giving. In a marriage, it means seeking to give of our whole selves: body, soul, and spirit.

First, Remember: Marriage Has Deep Meaning

The "one flesh" experience should be an expression and a heightening of the partners' sense that, being given to each other, they now belong together, each needing the other for completion and wholeness.

—J. I. Packer[1]

Ye have heard that it was said by them of old time, Thou shalt not commit adultery:

But I say unto you, That whosoever looketh on a woman to lust after her hath committed adultery with her already in his heart.

And if thy right eye offend thee, pluck it out, and cast it from thee: for it is profitable for thee that one of thy members should perish, and not that thy whole body should be cast into hell.

And if thy right hand offend thee, cut it off, and cast it from thee: for it is profitable for thee that one of thy members should perish, and not that thy whole body should be cast into hell.

It hath been said, Whosoever shall put away his wife, let him give her a writing of divorcement:

But I say unto you, That whosoever shall put away his wife, saving for the cause of fornication, causeth her to commit adultery: and whosoever shall marry her that is divorced committeth adultery.

—*Matthew 5:27–32*

Marriage is honourable in all, and the bed undefiled.

—*Hebrews 13:4a*

Let us be glad and rejoice, and give honour to him: for the marriage of the Lamb is come, and his wife hath made herself ready.

And to her was granted that she should be arrayed in fine linen, clean and white: for the fine linen is the righteousness of saints.

And he saith unto me, Write, Blessed are they which are called unto the marriage supper of the Lamb. And he saith unto me, These are the true sayings of God.

—Revelation 19:7–9

Do the Things that Strengthen a Marriage

A wedding is not a marriage. A wedding is only the beginning of an undertaking that may or may not, someday, develop into a marriage. What the couple have on their wedding day is not the key to a beautiful garden, but just a vacant lot and a few gardening tools.

—David and Vera Mace[2]

Let thy fountain be blessed: and rejoice with the wife of thy youth.

Let her be as the loving hind and pleasant roe; let her breasts satisfy thee at all times; and be thou ravished always with her love.

And why wilt thou, my son, be ravished with a strange woman, and embrace the bosom of a stranger?

—Proverbs 5:18–20

Live joyfully with the wife whom thou lovest all the days of the life of thy vanity, which he hath given thee under the sun, all the days of thy vanity: for that is thy portion in this life, and in thy labour which thou takest under the sun.

—*Ecclesiastes 9:9*

The voice of my beloved! behold, he cometh leaping upon the mountains, skipping upon the hills.

My beloved is like a roe or a young hart: behold, he standeth behind our wall, he looketh forth at the windows, shewing himself through the lattice.

My beloved spake, and said unto me, Rise up, my love, my fair one, and come away.

For, lo, the winter is past, the rain is over and gone;

The flowers appear on the earth; the time of the singing of birds is come, and the voice of the turtle is heard in our land;

The fig tree putteth forth her green figs, and the vines with the tender grape give a good smell. Arise, my love, my fair one, and come away.

—Song of Solomon 2:8–13

My beloved is white and ruddy, the chiefest among ten thousand.

His head is as the most fine gold, his locks are bushy, and black as a raven.

His eyes are as the eyes of doves by the rivers of waters, washed with milk, and fitly set.

His cheeks are as a bed of spices, as sweet flowers: his lips like lilies, dropping sweet smelling myrrh.

His hands are as gold rings set with the beryl: his belly is as bright ivory overlaid with sapphires.

His legs are as pillars of marble, set upon sockets of fine gold: his countenance is as Lebanon, excellent as the cedars.

His mouth is most sweet: yea, he is altogether lovely. This is my beloved, and this is my friend, O daughters of Jerusalem.

—Song of Solomon 5:10–16

Learn from These Poor Marriages

Your home can be a place for dying or living, for wilting or blooming, for anxiety or peace, for discouragement or affirmation, for criticism or approval, for profane disregard or reverence, for suspicion or trust, for blame or forgiveness, for alienation or closeness, for violation or respect, for carelessness or caring. By your daily choices, you will make your home what you want it to be.

—Carole Streeter[3]

❤ *Solomon—Compromising His Convictions*

But king Solomon loved many strange women, together with the daughter of Pharaoh, women of the Moabites, Ammonites, Edomites, Zidonians, and Hittites;

Of the nations concerning which the LORD said unto the children of Israel, Ye shall not go in to them, neither shall they come in unto you: for surely they will turn away your heart after their gods: Solomon clave unto these in love.

And he had seven hundred wives, princesses, and three hundred concubines: and his wives turned away his heart.

For it came to pass, when Solomon was old, that his wives turned away his heart after other gods: and his heart was not perfect with the LORD his God, as was the heart of David his father.

For Solomon went after Ashtoreth the goddess of the Zidonians, and after Milcom the abomination of the Ammonites.

And Solomon did evil in the sight of the LORD, and went not fully after the LORD, as did David his father.

Then did Solomon build an high place for Chemosh, the abomination of Moab, in the hill that is before Jerusalem, and for Molech, the abomination of the children of Ammon.

And likewise did he for all his strange wives, which burnt incense and sacrificed unto their gods.

And the LORD was angry with Solomon, because his heart was turned from the LORD God of Israel, which had appeared unto him twice,

And had commanded him concerning this thing, that he should not go after other gods: but he kept not that which the LORD commanded.

Wherefore the LORD said unto Solomon, Forasmuch as this is done of thee, and thou hast not kept my covenant and my statutes, which I have commanded thee, I will surely rend the kingdom from thee, and will give it to thy servant.

Notwithstanding in thy days I will not do it for David thy father's sake: but I will rend it out of the hand of thy son.

—1 Kings 11:1–12

❤ *Herod and Herodias— Behind Each Other's Backs*

Is not this the carpenter, the son of Mary, the brother of James, and Joses, and of Juda, and Simon? and are not his sisters here with us? And they were offended at him.

But Jesus said unto them, A prophet is not without honour, but in his own country, and among his own kin, and in his own house. . . .

And king Herod heard of him; (for his name was spread abroad:) and he said, That John the Baptist was risen from the dead, and therefore mighty works do shew forth themselves in him.

Others said, That it is Elias. And others said, That it is a prophet, or as one of the prophets.

But when Herod heard thereof, he said, It is John, whom I beheaded: he is risen from the dead.

For Herod himself had sent forth and laid hold upon John, and bound him in prison for Herodias' sake, his brother Philip's wife: for he had married her.

For John had said unto Herod, It is not lawful for thee to have thy brother's wife.

Therefore Herodias had a quarrel against him, and would have killed him; but she could not:

For Herod feared John, knowing that he was a just man and an holy, and observed him; and when he heard him, he did many things, and heard him gladly.

And when a convenient day was come, that Herod on his birthday made a supper to his lords, high captains, and chief estates of Galilee;

And when the daughter of the said Herodias came in, and danced, and pleased Herod and them that sat with him, the king said unto the damsel, Ask of me whatsoever thou wilt, and I will give it thee.

And he sware unto her, Whatsoever thou shalt ask of me, I will give it thee, unto the half of my kingdom.

And she went forth, and said unto her mother, What shall I ask? And she said, The head of John the Baptist.

And she came in straightway with haste unto the king, and asked, saying, I will that thou give me by and by in a charger the head of John the Baptist.

And the king was exceeding sorry; yet for his oath's sake, and for their sakes which sat with him, he would not reject her.

And immediately the king sent an executioner, and commanded his head to be brought: and he went and beheaded him in the prison,

And brought his head in a charger, and gave it to the damsel: and the damsel gave it to her mother.

—Mark 6:3–4, 14–28

❤ *Samson and Delilah—Nagging Dishonesty*

And it came to pass afterward, that he loved a woman in the valley of Sorek, whose name was Delilah.

And the lords of the Philistines came up unto her, and said unto her, Entice him, and see wherein his great strength lieth, and by what means we may prevail against him, that we may bind him to afflict him: and we will give thee every one of us eleven hundred pieces of silver.

And Delilah said to Samson, Tell me, I pray thee, wherein thy great strength lieth, and wherewith thou mightest be bound to afflict thee.

And Samson said unto her, If they bind me with seven green withs that were never dried, then shall I be weak, and be as another man.

Then the lords of the Philistines brought up to her seven green withs which had not been dried, and she bound him with them.

Now there were men lying in wait, abiding with her in the chamber. And she said unto him, The Philistines be upon thee, Samson. And he brake the withs, as a thread of tow is broken when it toucheth the fire. So his strength was not known.

And Delilah said unto Samson, Behold, thou hast mocked me, and told me lies: now tell me, I pray thee, wherewith thou mightest be bound.

And he said unto her, If they bind me fast with new ropes that never were occupied, then shall I be weak, and be as another man.

Delilah therefore took new ropes, and bound him therewith, and said unto him, The Philistines be upon thee, Samson. And there were liers in wait abiding in the chamber. And he brake them from off his arms like a thread.

And Delilah said unto Samson, Hitherto thou hast mocked me, and told me lies: tell me wherewith thou mightest be bound. And he said unto her, If thou weavest the seven locks of my head with the web.

And she fastened it with the pin, and said unto him, The Philistines be upon thee, Samson. And he awaked out of his sleep, and went away with the pin of the beam, and with the web.

And she said unto him, How canst thou say, I love thee, when thine heart is not with me? thou hast mocked me these three times, and hast not told me wherein thy great strength lieth.

And it came to pass, when she pressed him daily with her words, and urged him, so that his soul was vexed unto death;

That he told her all his heart, and said unto her, There hath not come a razor upon mine head; for I have been a Nazarite unto God from my mother's womb: if I be shaven, then my strength will go from me, and I shall become weak, and be like any other man.

And when Delilah saw that he had told her all his heart, she sent and called for the lords of the Philistines, saying, Come up this once, for he hath shewed me all his heart. Then the lords of the Philistines came up unto her, and brought money in their hand.

And she made him sleep upon her knees; and she called for a man, and she caused him to shave off the seven locks of his head; and she began to afflict him, and his strength went from him.

—Judges 16:4–19

❤ *Ahab and Jezebel—Wrongful Places*

And in the thirty and eighth year of Asa king of Judah began Ahab the son of Omri to reign over Israel: and Ahab the son of Omri reigned over Israel in Samaria twenty and two years.

And Ahab the son of Omri did evil in the sight of the LORD above all that were before him.

And it came to pass, as if it had been a light thing for him to walk in the sins of Jeroboam the son of Nebat, that he took to wife Jezebel the daughter of Ethbaal king of the Zidonians, and went and served Baal, and worshipped him.

And he reared up an altar for Baal in the house of Baal, which he had built in Samaria.

And Ahab made a grove; and Ahab did more to provoke the LORD God of Israel to anger than all the kings of Israel that were before him.

—1 Kings 16:29–33

Run from Sexual Temptation

Our old man is crucified, but he is long a-dying.

—Charles Spurgeon

It came to pass after these things, that his master's wife cast her eyes upon Joseph; and she said, Lie with me.

But he refused, and said unto his master's wife, Behold, my master wotteth not what is with me in the house, and he hath committed all that he hath to my hand;

There is none greater in this house than I; neither hath he kept back any thing from me but thee, because thou art his wife: how then can I do this great wickedness, and sin against God?

And it came to pass, as she spake to Joseph day by day, that he hearkened not unto her, to lie by her, or to be with her.

And it came to pass about this time, that Joseph went into the house to do his business; and there was none of the men of the house there within.

And she caught him by his garment, saying, Lie with me: and he left his garment in her hand, and fled, and got him out.

—Genesis 39:7–12

Flee fornication. Every sin that a man doeth is without the body; but he that committeth fornication sinneth against his own body.

What? know ye not that your body is the temple of the Holy Ghost which is in you, which ye have of God, and ye are not your own?

For ye are bought with a price: therefore glorify God in your body, and in your spirit, which are God's.

—1 Corinthians 6:18–20

Submit yourselves therefore to God. Resist the devil, and he will flee from you.

Draw nigh to God, and he will draw nigh to you. Cleanse your hands, ye sinners; and purify your hearts, ye double minded.

—James 4:7–8

For the weapons of our warfare are not carnal, but mighty through God to the pulling down of strong holds.

—2 Corinthians 10:4

But in a great house there are not only vessels of gold and of silver, but also of wood and of earth; and some to honour, and some to dishonour.

If a man therefore purge himself from these, he shall be a vessel unto honour, sanctified, and meet for the master's use, and prepared unto every good work.

Flee also youthful lusts: but follow righteousness, faith, charity, peace, with them that call on the Lord out of a pure heart.

—2 Timothy 2:20–22

Put on the whole armour of God, that ye may be able to stand against the wiles of the devil.

For we wrestle not against flesh and blood, but against principalities, against powers, against the rulers of the darkness of this world, against spiritual wickedness in high places.

Wherefore take unto you the whole armour of God, that ye may be able to withstand in the evil day, and having done all, to stand.

Stand therefore, having your loins girt about with truth, and having on the breastplate of righteousness.

—*Ephesians 6:11–14*

Blessed is the man that endureth temptation: for when he is tried, he shall receive the crown of life, which the Lord hath promised to them that love him.

—*James 1:12*

Neither give place to the devil.

—*Ephesians 4.27*

❤ *Your Conscience Can Be Your Guide*

For our rejoicing is this, the testimony of our conscience, that in simplicity and godly sincerity, not with fleshly wisdom, but by the grace of God, we have had our conversation in the world, and more abundantly to you-ward.

—2 Corinthians 1:12

Having a good conscience; that, whereas they speak evil of you, as of evildoers, they may be ashamed that falsely accuse your good conversation in Christ. . . .

The like figure whereunto even baptism doth also now save us (not the putting away of the filth of the flesh, but the answer of a good conscience toward God,) by the resurrection of Jesus Christ.

—1 Peter 3:16, 21

Now the end of the commandment is charity out of a pure heart, and of a good conscience, and of faith unfeigned.

—1 Timothy 1:5

Holding the mystery of the faith in a pure conscience.

—1 Timothy 3:9

❤ *Learn Temptation's Tricks*

Then was Jesus led up of the Spirit into the wilderness to be tempted of the devil.

And when he had fasted forty days and forty nights, he was afterward an hungered.

And when the tempter came to him, he said, If thou be the Son of God, command that these stones be made bread.

But he answered and said, It is written, Man shall not live by bread alone, but by every word that proceedeth out of the mouth of God.

Then the devil taketh him up into the holy city, and setteth him on a pinnacle of the temple,

And saith unto him, If thou be the Son of God, cast thyself down: for it is written, He shall give his angels charge concerning thee: and in their hands they shall bear thee up, lest at any time thou dash thy foot against a stone.

Jesus said unto him, It is written again, Thou shalt not tempt the Lord thy God.

Again, the devil taketh him up into an exceeding high mountain, and sheweth him all the kingdoms of the world, and the glory of them;

And saith unto him, All these things will I give thee, if thou wilt fall down and worship me.

Then saith Jesus unto him, Get thee hence, Satan: for it is written, Thou shalt worship the Lord thy God, and him only shalt thou serve.

Then the devil leaveth him, and, behold, angels came and ministered unto him.

—*Matthew 4:1–11*

Watch therefore: for ye know not what hour your Lord doth come.

But know this, that if the goodman of the house had known in what watch the thief would come, he would have watched, and would not have suffered his house to be broken up.

—*Matthew 24:42–44*

For the lips of a strange woman drop as an honeycomb, and her mouth is smoother than oil:

But her end is bitter as wormwood, sharp as a twoedged sword.

Her feet go down to death; her steps take hold on hell.

Lest thou shouldest ponder the path of life, her ways are moveable, that thou canst not know them.

Hear me now therefore, O ye children, and depart not from the words of my mouth.

Remove thy way far from her, and come not nigh the door of her house:

Lest thou give thine honour unto others, and thy years unto the cruel:

Lest strangers be filled with thy wealth; and thy labours be in the house of a stranger;

And thou mourn at the last, when thy flesh and thy body are consumed,

And say, How have I hated instruction, and my heart despised reproof;

And have not obeyed the voice of my teachers, nor inclined mine ear to them that instructed me!

I was almost in all evil in the midst of the congregation and assembly.

—Proverbs 5:3–14

For at the window of my house I looked through my casement,

And beheld among the simple ones, I discerned among the youths, a young man void of understanding,

Passing through the street near her corner; and he went the way to her house,

In the twilight, in the evening, in the black and dark night:

And, behold, there met him a woman with the attire of an harlot, and subtil of heart.

(She is loud and stubborn; her feet abide not in her house:

Now is she without, now in the streets, and lieth in wait at every corner.)

So she caught him, and kissed him, and with an impudent face said unto him,

I have peace offerings with me; this day have I payed my vows.

Therefore came I forth to meet thee, diligently to seek thy face, and I have found thee.

I have decked my bed with coverings of tapestry, with carved works, with fine linen of Egypt.

I have perfumed my bed with myrrh, aloes, and cinnamon.

Come, let us take our fill of love until the morning: let us solace ourselves with loves.

For the goodman is not at home, he is gone a long journey:

He hath taken a bag of money with him, and will come home at the day appointed.

With her much fair speech she caused him to yield, with the flattering of her lips she forced him.

He goeth after her straightway, as an ox goeth to the slaughter, or as a fool to the correction of the stocks;

Till a dart strike through his liver; as a bird hasteth to the snare, and knoweth not that it is for his life.

Hearken unto me now therefore, O ye children, and attend to the words of my mouth.

Let not thine heart decline to her ways, go not astray in her paths.

For she hath cast down many wounded: yea, many strong men have been slain by her.

Her house is the way to hell, going down to the chambers of death.

—Proverbs 7:6–27

❤ *Depend on God to Carry You Through It*

He giveth power to the faint; and to them that have no might he increaseth strength.

Even the youths shall faint and be weary, and the young men shall utterly fall:

But they that wait upon the LORD shall renew their strength; they shall mount up with wings as eagles; they shall run, and not be weary; and they shall walk, and not faint.

—Isaiah 40:29–31

There hath no temptation taken you but such as is common to man: but God is faithful, who will not suffer you to be tempted above that ye are able; but will with the temptation also make a way to escape, that ye may be able to bear it.

—1 Corinthians 10:13

But the Lord is faithful, who shall stablish you, and keep you from evil.

—2 Thessalonians 3:3

And the Lord shall deliver me from every evil work, and will preserve me unto his heavenly kingdom: to whom be glory for ever and ever. Amen.

—2 Timothy 4:18

Forasmuch then as the children are partakers of flesh and blood, he also himself likewise took part of the same; that through death he might destroy him that had the power of death, that is, the devil;

And deliver them who through fear of death were all their lifetime subject to bondage.

For verily he took not on him the nature of angels; but he took on him the seed of Abraham.

Wherefore in all things it behoved him to be made like unto his brethren, that he might be a merciful and faithful high priest in things pertaining to God, to make reconciliation for the sins of the people.

For in that he himself hath suffered being tempted, he is able to succour them that are tempted.

Wherefore, holy brethren, partakers of the heavenly calling, consider the Apostle and High Priest of our profession, Christ Jesus.

—*Hebrews 2:14–18; 3:1*

When thou goest, thy steps shall not be straitened; and when thou runnest, thou shalt not stumble.

—*Proverbs 4:12*

Ask, and it shall be given you; seek, and ye shall find; knock, and it shall be opened unto you.

—*Matthew 7:7*

I beseech you therefore, brethren, by the mercies of God, that ye present your bodies a living sacrifice, holy, acceptable unto God, which is your reasonable service.

—*Romans 12:1*

—Seven—

Money Matters

It's easy to say, "Don't worry about money!" But how successful are you at squelching the twinges of doubt, especially late at night when you wake up and think about those bills? How are you ever going to make ends meet, month after month? Recognize that worry about anything never helps. Set your budget, live within it at all costs, make the wisest decisions you can, and give your worries to the Lord.

Don't Worry about Your Finances!

Riches are the pettiest and least worthy gifts which God can give a man. What are they to God's Word, to bodily gifts, such as beauty and health; or to the gifts of the mind, such as understanding, skill, wisdom? Yet men toil for them day and night, and take not rest. Therefore God commonly gives riches to foolish people to whom he gives nothing else.

—Martin Luther

Thou wilt keep him in perfect peace, whose mind is stayed on thee: because he trusteth in thee.

Trust ye in the LORD for ever: for in the LORD JEHOVAH is everlasting strength:

—Isaiah 26:3–4

For every beast of the forest is mine, and the cattle upon a thousand hills.

I know all the fowls of the mountains: and the wild beasts of the field are mine.

If I were hungry, I would not tell thee: for the world is mine, and the fulness thereof.

Will I eat the flesh of bulls, or drink the blood of goats?

Offer unto God thanksgiving; and pay thy vows unto the most High:

And call upon me in the day of trouble: I will deliver thee, and thou shalt glorify me.

—Psalm 50:10–15

These things I have spoken unto you, that in me ye might have peace. In the world ye shall have tribulation: but be of good cheer; I have overcome the world.

—John 16:33

For he shall be as a tree planted by the waters, and that spreadeth out her roots by the river, and shall not see when heat cometh, but her leaf shall be green; and shall not be careful in the year of drought, neither shall cease from yielding fruit.

—Jeremiah 17:8

And the peace of God, which passeth all understanding, shall keep your hearts and minds through Christ Jesus.

—Philippians 4:7

Now the Lord of peace himself give you peace always by all means. The Lord be with you all.

—2 Thessalonians 3:16

❤ *Practice Good Stewardship*

John answered and said, A man can receive nothing, except it be given him from heaven.

—John 3:27

The earth is the LORD'S, and the fulness thereof; the world, and they that dwell therein.

For he hath founded it upon the seas, and established it upon the floods.

—Psalm 24:1–2

Behold, the heaven and the heaven of heavens is the LORD's thy God, the earth also, with all that therein is.

—Deuteronomy 10:14

Upon the first day of the week let every one of you lay by him in store, as God hath prospered him, that there be no gatherings when I come.

—1 Corinthians 16:2

Cast thy bread upon the waters: for thou shalt find it after many days.

—Ecclesiastes 11:1

Give, and it shall be given unto you; good measure, pressed down, and shaken together, and running over, shall men give into your bosom. For with the same measure that ye mete withal it shall be measured to you again.

—Luke 6:38

Will a man rob God? Yet ye have robbed me. But ye say, Wherein have we robbed thee? In tithes and offerings.

Ye are cursed with a curse: for ye have robbed me, even this whole nation.

Bring ye all the tithes into the storehouse, that there may be meat in mine house, and prove me now herewith, saith the LORD of hosts, if I will not open you the windows of heaven, and pour you out a blessing, that there shall not be room enough to receive it.

And I will rebuke the devourer for your sakes, and he shall not destroy the fruits of your ground; neither shall your vine cast her fruit before the time in the field, saith the LORD of hosts.

And all nations shall call you blessed: for ye shall be a delightsome land, saith the LORD of hosts.

—*Malachi 3:8–12*

But this I say, He which soweth sparingly shall reap also sparingly; and he which soweth bountifully shall reap also bountifully.

Every man according as he purposeth in his heart, so let him give; not grudgingly, or of necessity: for God loveth a cheerful giver.

And God is able to make all grace abound toward you; that ye, always having all sufficiency in all things, may abound to every good work:

(As it is written, He hath dispersed abroad; he hath given to the poor: his righteousness remaineth for ever.

Now he that ministereth seed to the sower both minister bread for your food, and multiply your seed sown, and increase the fruits of your righteousness;)

Being enriched in every thing to all bountifulness, which causeth through us thanksgiving to God.

—2 Corinthians 9:6–11

And all the wise men, that wrought all the work of the sanctuary, came every man from his work which they made;

And they spake unto Moses, saying, The people bring much more than enough for the service of the work, which the LORD commanded to make.

And Moses gave commandment, and they caused it to be proclaimed throughout the camp, saying, Let neither man nor woman make any more work for the offering of the sanctuary. So the people were restrained from bringing.

For the stuff they had was sufficient for all the work to make it, and too much.

—Exodus 36:4–7

And as soon as the commandment came abroad, the children of Israel brought in abundance the firstfruits of corn, wine, and oil, and honey, and of all the increase of the field; and the tithe of all things brought they in abundantly.

And concerning the children of Israel and Judah, that dwelt in the cities of Judah, they also brought in the tithe of oxen and sheep, and the tithe of holy things which were consecrated unto the LORD their God, and laid them by heaps.

In the third month they began to lay the foundation of the heaps, and finished them in the seventh month.

And when Hezekiah and the princes came and saw the heaps, they blessed the LORD, and his people Israel.

—2 Chronicles 31:5–8

And Jesus entered and passed through Jericho.

And, behold, there was a man named Zacchaeus, which was the chief among the publicans, and he was rich.

And he sought to see Jesus who he was; and could not for the press, because he was little of stature.

And he ran before, and climbed up into a sycomore tree to see him: for he was to pass that way.

And when Jesus came to the place, he looked up, and saw him, and said unto him, Zacchaeus, make haste, and come down; for to day I must abide at thy house.

And he made haste, and came down, and received him joyfully.

And when they saw it, they all murmured, saying, That he was gone to be guest with a man that is a sinner.

And Zacchaeus stood, and said unto the Lord; Behold, Lord, the half of my goods I give to the poor; and if I have taken any thing from any man by false accusation, I restore him fourfold.

And Jesus said unto him, This day is salvation come to this house, forsomuch as he also is a son of Abraham.

For the Son of man is come to seek and to save that which was lost.

—*Luke 19:1–10*

And when James, Cephas, and John, who seemed to be pillars, perceived the grace that was given unto me, they gave to me and Barnabas the right hands of fellowship; that we should go unto the heathen, and they unto the circumcision.

Only they would that we should remember the poor; the same which I also was forward to do.

—*Galatians 2:9–10*

For I mean not that other men be eased, and ye burdened:

But by an equality, that now at this time your abundance may be a supply for their want, that their abundance also may be a supply for your want: that there may be equality:

As it is written, He that had gathered much had nothing over; and he that had gathered little had no lack.

—2 Corinthians 8:13–15

Charge them that are rich in this world, that they be not highminded, nor trust in uncertain riches, but in the living God, who giveth us richly all things to enjoy;

That they do good, that they be rich in good works, ready to distribute, willing to communicate;

Laying up in store for themselves a good foundation against the time to come, that they may lay hold on eternal life.

—1 Timothy 6:17–19

As every man hath received the gift, even so minister the same one to another, as good stewards of the manifold grace of God.

If any man speak, let him speak as the oracles of God; if any man minister, let him do it as of the ability which God giveth: that God in all things may be glorified through

Jesus Christ, to whom be praise and dominion for ever and ever. Amen.

—1 Peter 4:10–11

❤ *Practice Frugality*

And he gathered up all the food of the seven years, which were in the land of Egypt, and laid up the food in the cities: the food of the field, which was round about every city, laid he up in the same.

And Joseph gathered corn as the sand of the sea, very much, until he left numbering; for it was without number.

And unto Joseph were born two sons before the years of famine came, which Asenath the daughter of Poti-pherah priest of On bare unto him.

And Joseph called the name of the firstborn Manasseh: For God, said he, hath made me forget all my toil, and all my father's house.

And the name of the second called he Ephraim: For God hath caused me to be fruitful in the land of my affliction.

And the seven years of plenteousness, that was in the land of Egypt, were ended.

And the seven years of dearth began to come, according as Joseph had said: and the dearth was in all lands; but in all the land of Egypt there was bread.

—Genesis 41:48–54

And the children of Israel did so, and gathered, some more, some less.

And when they did mete it with an omer, he that gathered much had nothing over, and he that gathered little had no lack; they gathered every man according to his eating.

And Moses said, Let no man leave of it till the morning.

Notwithstanding they hearkened not unto Moses; but some of them left of it until the morning, and it bred worms, and stank: and Moses was wroth with them.

And they gathered it every morning, every man according to his eating: and when the sun waxed hot, it melted.

And it came to pass, that on the sixth day they gathered twice as much bread, two omers for one man: and all the rulers of the congregation came and told Moses.

And he said unto them, This is that which the LORD hath said, To morrow is the rest of the holy sabbath unto the LORD: bake that which ye will bake to day, and seethe that ye will seethe; and that which remaineth over lay up for you to be kept until the morning.

And they laid it up till the morning, as Moses bade: and it did not stink, neither was there any worm therein.

—Exodus 16:17–24

So he went and did according unto the word of the LORD: for he went and dwelt by the brook Cherith, that is before Jordan.

And the ravens brought him bread and flesh in the morning, and bread and flesh in the evening; and he drank of the brook.

And it came to pass after a while, that the brook dried up, because there had been no rain in the land.

And the word of the LORD came unto him, saying,

Arise, get thee to Zarephath, which belongeth to Zidon, and dwell there: behold, I have commanded a widow woman there to sustain thee.

So he arose and went to Zarephath. And when he came to the gate of the city, behold, the widow woman was there gathering of sticks: and he called to her, and said, Fetch me, I pray thee, a little water in a vessel, that I may drink.

And as she was going to fetch it, he called to her, and said, Bring me, I pray thee, a morsel of bread in thine hand.

And she said, As the LORD thy God liveth, I have not a cake, but an handful of meal in a barrel, and a little oil in a cruse: and, behold, I am gathering two sticks, that I may go in and dress it for me and my son, that we may eat it, and die.

And Elijah said unto her, Fear not; go and do as thou hast said: but make me thereof a little cake first, and bring it unto me, and after make for thee and for thy son.

—1 Kings 17:5–13

A good man leaveth an inheritance to his children's children: and the wealth of the sinner is laid up for the just.

—*Proverbs 13:22*

He that loveth pleasure shall be a poor man: he that loveth wine and oil shall not be rich. . . .

There is treasure to be desired and oil in the dwelling of the wise; but a foolish man spendeth it up.

—*Proverbs 21:17, 20*

Be not among winebibbers; among riotous eaters of flesh:

For the drunkard and the glutton shall come to poverty: and drowsiness shall clothe a man with rags.

—*Proverbs 23:20–21*

Approach Your Work with Joy

We pray for the strength to go to work every day. It's not easy to get up early and then go out to face the world. The competition is tough, the bottom line inflexible. Give us the strength to work!

—Gary Wilde[1]

Commit thy works unto the LORD, and thy thoughts shall be established.

—Proverbs 16:3

But none of these things move me, neither count I my life dear unto myself, so that I might finish my course with joy, and the ministry, which I have received of the Lord Jesus, to testify the gospel of the grace of God.

—Acts 20:24

But we have this treasure in earthen vessels, that the excellency of the power may be of God, and not of us.

We are troubled on every side, yet not distressed; we are perplexed, but not in despair;

Persecuted, but not forsaken; cast down, but not destroyed;

Always bearing about in the body the dying of the Lord Jesus, that the life also of Jesus might be made manifest in our body.

For we which live are alway delivered unto death for Jesus' sake, that the life also of Jesus might be made manifest in our mortal flesh.

—2 Corinthians 4:7–11

Remember: It's Good to Work Hard

How boring these meaningless details!
Is this really what work is meant to be?
Can You make it sing again?
Put the spark back in my zeal?
Because I know that work is a blessed privilege;
I don't want to be ungrateful.

But how boring the piles of paperwork,
how deadening the countless reports,
how fatiguing the endless round of meetings.
Yes, I need to feel it again, Lord—the joy.

—Gary Wilde[2]

He that tilleth his land shall be satisfied with bread: but he that followeth vain persons is void of understanding. . . .

The hand of the diligent shall bear rule: but the slothful shall be under tribute.

Heaviness in the heart of man maketh it stoop: but a good word maketh it glad.

The righteous is more excellent than his neighbour: but the way of the wicked seduceth them.

The slothful man roasteth not that which he took in hunting: but the substance of a diligent man is precious.

—Proverbs 12:11, 24–27

Be thou diligent to know the state of thy flocks, and look well to thy herds.

For riches are not for ever: and doth the crown endure to every generation?

The hay appeareth, and the tender grass sheweth itself, and herbs of the mountains are gathered.

The lambs are for thy clothing, and the goats are the price of the field.

And thou shalt have goats' milk enough for thy food, for the food of thy household, and for the maintenance for thy maidens.

—*Proverbs 27:23–27*

The ants are a people not strong, yet they prepare their meat in the summer;

The conies are but a feeble folk, yet make they their houses in the rocks;

The locusts have no king, yet go they forth all of them by bands;

The spider taketh hold with her hands, and is in kings' palaces.

—*Proverbs 30:25–28*

I have coveted no man's silver, or gold, or apparel.

Yea, ye yourselves know, that these hands have ministered unto my necessities, and to them that were with me.

—*Acts 20:33–34*

For even when we were with you, this we commanded you, that if any would not work, neither should he eat.

For we hear that there are some which walk among you disorderly, working not at all, but are busybodies.

Now them that are such we command and exhort by our Lord Jesus Christ, that with quietness they work, and eat their own bread.

—2 Thessalonians 3:10–12

And that ye study to be quiet, and to do your own business, and to work with your own hands, as we commanded you;

That ye may walk honestly toward them that are without, and that ye may have lack of nothing.

—1 Thessalonians 4:11–12

—Eight—

Are You Ready for Parenting?

It could happen, you know. So it's something to think about even now: the prospect of little ones. How would you handle that? What would your new family be like? Read on for some heavenly suggestions.

Cherish the Prospect of Children

God hangs the greatest weights upon the smallest wires.

—Francis Bacon

Lo, children are an heritage of the LORD: and the fruit of the womb is his reward.

As arrows are in the hand of a mighty man; so are children of the youth.

Happy is the man that hath his quiver full of them: they shall not be ashamed, but they shall speak with the enemies in the gate.

—Psalm 127:3–5

Whosoever therefore shall humble himself as this little child, the same is greatest in the kingdom of heaven.

And whoso shall receive one such little child in my name receiveth me. . . .

Take heed that ye despise not one of these little ones; for I say unto you, That in heaven their angels do always behold the face of my Father which is in heaven.

—Matthew 18:4–5, 10

And they brought young children to him, that he should touch them: and his disciples rebuked those that brought them.

But when Jesus saw it, he was much displeased, and said unto them, Suffer the little children to come unto me, and forbid them not: for of such is the kingdom of God.

Verily I say unto you, Whosoever shall not receive the kingdom of God as a little child, he shall not enter therein.

And he took them up in his arms, put his hands upon them, and blessed them.

—Mark 10:13–16

And said unto them, Whosoever shall receive this child in my name receiveth me: and whosoever shall receive me receiveth him that sent me: for he that is least among you all, the same shall be great.

—Luke 9:48

In that hour Jesus rejoiced in spirit, and said, I thank thee, O Father, Lord of heaven and earth, that thou hast hid these things from the wise and prudent, and hast revealed them unto babes: even so, Father; for so it seemed good in thy sight.

—Luke 10:21

And when the chief priests and scribes saw the wonderful things that he did, and the children crying in the temple, and saying, Hosanna to the Son of David; they were sore displeased,

And said unto him, Hearest thou what these say? And Jesus saith unto them, Yea; have ye never read, Out of the mouth of babes and sucklings thou hast perfected praise?

—Matthew 21:15–16

He shall feed his flock like a shepherd: he shall gather the lambs with his arm, and carry them in his bosom, and shall gently lead those that are with young.

—Isaiah 40:11

Dedicate Your Infant to God

We've had bad luck with our kids—they've all grown up.

—Christopher Morley

And the man Elkanah, and all his house, went up to offer unto the LORD the yearly sacrifice, and his vow.

But Hannah went not up; for she said unto her husband, I will not go up until the child be weaned, and then I will bring him, that he may appear before the LORD, and there abide for ever.

And Elkanah her husband said unto her, Do what seemeth thee good; tarry until thou have weaned him; only the LORD establish his word. So the woman abode, and gave her son suck until she weaned him.

And when she had weaned him, she took him up with her, with three bullocks, and one ephah of flour, and a bottle of wine, and brought him unto the house of the LORD in Shiloh: and the child was young.

And they slew a bullock, and brought the child to Eli.

And she said, Oh my lord, as thy soul liveth, my lord, I am the woman that stood by thee here, praying unto the LORD.

For this child I prayed; and the LORD hath given me my petition which I asked of him:

Therefore also I have lent him to the LORD; as long as he liveth he shall be lent to the LORD. And he worshipped the LORD there.

—1 Samuel 1:21–28

And when eight days were accomplished for the circumcising of the child, his name was called JESUS, which was so named of the angel before he was conceived in the womb.

And when the days of her purification according to the law of Moses were accomplished, they brought him to Jerusalem, to present him to the Lord;

(As it is written in the law of the Lord, Every male that openeth the womb shall be called holy to the Lord;)

And to offer a sacrifice according to that which is said in the law of the Lord, A pair of turtledoves, or two young pigeons.

And, behold, there was a man in Jerusalem, whose name was Simeon; and the same man was just and devout, waiting for the consolation of Israel: and the Holy Ghost was upon him.

And it was revealed unto him by the Holy Ghost, that he should not see death, before he had seen the Lord's Christ.

And he came by the Spirit into the temple: and when the parents brought in the child Jesus, to do for him after the custom of the law,

Then took he him up in his arms, and blessed God, and said,

Lord, now lettest thou thy servant depart in peace, according to thy word:

For mine eyes have seen thy salvation,

Which thou hast prepared before the face of all people;

A light to lighten the Gentiles, and the glory of thy people Israel.

And Joseph and his mother marvelled at those things which were spoken of him.

—Luke 2:21–33

❤ *Pray for Your Newborn*

And Abraham said unto God, O that Ishmael might live before thee!

—Genesis 17:18

And now, O LORD God, the word that thou hast spoken concerning thy servant, and concerning his house, establish it for ever, and do as thou hast said.

And let thy name be magnified for ever, saying, The LORD of hosts is the God over Israel: and let the house of thy servant David be established before thee.

For thou, O LORD of hosts, God of Israel, hast revealed to thy servant, saying, I will build thee an house: therefore hath thy servant found in his heart to pray this prayer unto thee.

And now, O Lord GOD, thou art that God, and thy words be true, and thou hast promised this goodness unto thy servant:

Therefore now let it please thee to bless the house of thy servant, that it may continue for ever before thee: for thou, O Lord GOD, hast spoken it: and with thy blessing let the house of thy servant be blessed for ever.

—2 Samuel 7:25–29

And it was so, when the days of their feasting were gone about, that Job sent and sanctified them, and rose up early in the morning, and offered burnt offerings according to the number of them all: for Job said, It may be that my sons have sinned, and cursed God in their hearts. Thus did Job continually.

—Job 1:5

❤ *Bestow Blessings on Your Children*

And Israel beheld Joseph's sons, and said, Who are these?

And Joseph said unto his father, They are my sons, whom God hath given me in this place. And he said, Bring them, I pray thee, unto me, and I will bless them.

Now the eyes of Israel were dim for age, so that he could not see. And he brought them near unto him; and he kissed them, and embraced them.

And Israel said unto Joseph, I had not thought to see thy face: and, lo, God hath shewed me also thy seed.

And Joseph brought them out from between his knees, and he bowed himself with his face to the earth.

And Joseph took them both, Ephraim in his right hand toward Israel's left hand, and Manasseh in his left hand toward Israel's right hand, and brought them near unto him.

And Israel stretched out his right hand, and laid it upon Ephraim's head, who was the younger, and his left hand upon Manasseh's head, guiding his hands wittingly; for Manasseh was the firstborn.

And he blessed Joseph, and said, God, before whom my fathers Abraham and Isaac did walk, the God which fed me all my life long unto this day,

The Angel which redeemed me from all evil, bless the lads; and let my name be named on them, and the name of my fathers Abraham and Isaac; and let them grow into a multitude in the midst of the earth.

—Genesis 48:8–16

Speak unto Aaron and unto his sons, saying, On this wise ye shall bless the children of Israel, saying unto them,

The LORD bless thee, and keep thee:

The LORD make his face shine upon thee, and be gracious unto thee:

The LORD lift up his countenance upon thee, and give thee peace.

—Numbers 6:23–26

And Naomi said unto her two daughters in law, Go, return each to her mother's house: the LORD deal kindly with you, as ye have dealt with the dead, and with me.

The LORD grant you that ye may find rest, each of you in the house of her husband.

Then she kissed them; and they lifted up their voice, and wept.

—*Ruth 1:8–9*

And he led them out as far as to Bethany, and he lifted up his hands, and blessed them.

And it came to pass, while he blessed them, he was parted from them, and carried up into heaven.

And they worshipped him, and returned to Jerusalem with great joy:

And were continually in the temple, praising and blessing God. Amen.

—*Luke 24:50–53*

❤ *Entrust Your Child to God's Care*

And all thy children shall be taught of the LORD; and great shall be the peace of thy children.

In righteousness shalt thou be established: thou shalt be far from oppression; for thou shalt not fear: and from terror; for it shall not come near thee.

—*Isaiah 54:13–14*

For, behold, I have made thee this day a defenced city, and an iron pillar, and brasen walls against the whole land, against the kings of Judah, against the princes thereof, against the priests thereof, and against the people of the land.

And they shall fight against thee; but they shall not prevail against thee; for I am with thee, saith the LORD, to deliver thee.

—Jeremiah 1:18–19

He that dwelleth in the secret place of the most High shall abide under the shadow of the Almighty.

I will say of the LORD, He is my refuge and my fortress: my God; in him will I trust.

Surely he shall deliver thee from the snare of the fowler, and from the noisome pestilence.

He shall cover thee with his feathers, and under his wings shalt thou trust: his truth shall be thy shield and buckler.

Thou shalt not be afraid for the terror by night; nor for the arrow that flieth by day;

Nor for the pestilence that walketh in darkness; nor for the destruction that wasteth at noonday.

A thousand shall fall at thy side, and ten thousand at thy right hand; but it shall not come nigh thee.

Only with thine eyes shalt thou behold and see the reward of the wicked.

Because thou hast made the LORD, which is my refuge, even the most High, thy habitation;

There shall no evil befall thee, neither shall any plague come nigh thy dwelling.

For he shall give his angels charge over thee, to keep thee in all thy ways.

They shall bear thee up in their hands, lest thou dash thy foot against a stone.

Thou shalt tread upon the lion and adder: the young lion and the dragon shalt thou trample under feet.

Because he hath set his love upon me, therefore will I deliver him: I will set him on high, because he hath known my name.

He shall call upon me, and I will answer him: I will be with him in trouble; I will deliver him, and honour him.

With long life will I satisfy him, and shew him my salvation.

—*Psalm 91:1–16*

Behold, I am the LORD, the God of all flesh: is there any thing too hard for me?

—*Jeremiah 32:27*

Keep Rejoicing in This Blessing from God

We should say to each of [our children]: Do you know what you are? You are a marvel. You are unique. In all the years that have passed, there has never been another child like you. Your legs, your arms, your clever fingers, the way you move. You may become a Shakespeare, a Michaelangelo, a Beethoven. You have the capacity for anything. Yes, you are a marvel. . . .

—*Pablo Casals*[1]

And God blessed them, saying, Be fruitful, and multiply.

—*Genesis 1:22a*

The LORD shall increase you more and more, you and your children.

Ye are blessed of the LORD which made heaven and earth.

The heaven, even the heavens, are the LORD's: but the earth hath he given to the children of men.

The dead praise not the LORD, neither any that go down into silence.

But we will bless the LORD from this time forth and for evermore. Praise the LORD.

—Psalm 115:14–18

He maketh the barren woman to keep house, and to be a joyful mother of children. Praise ye the LORD.

—Pslam 113:9

Every good gift and every perfect gift is from above, and cometh down from the Father of lights, with whom is no variableness, neither shadow of turning.

Of his own will begat he us with the word of truth, that we should be a kind of firstfruits of his creatures.

—James 1:17–18

The LORD is the portion of mine inheritance and of my cup: thou maintainest my lot.

The lines are fallen unto me in pleasant places; yea, I have a goodly heritage.

—Psalm 16:5–6

In every thing give thanks: for this is the will of God in Christ Jesus concerning you.

—1 Thessalonians 5:18

Sing, O ye heavens; for the LORD hath done it: shout, ye lower parts of the earth: break forth into singing, ye mountains, O forest, and every tree therein: for the LORD hath redeemed Jacob, and glorified himself in Israel.

—Isaiah 44:23

Raise Your Child in God's Ways

Americans once expected parents to raise their children in accordance with the

dominant cultural messages. Today they are expected to raise their children in opposition to them. Once the chorus of cultural values was full of ministers, teachers, neighbors, leaders. They demanded more conformity, but offered more support. Now the messengers are violent cartoon characters, rappers and celebrities selling sneakers.

—Ellen Goodman[2]

My little children, these things write I unto you, that ye sin not. And if any man sin, we have an advocate with the Father, Jesus Christ the righteous:

And he is the propitiation for our sins: and not for ours only, but also for the sins of the whole world. . . .

I write unto you, little children, because your sins are forgiven you for his name's sake.

—1 John 2:1–2, 12

For as many as are led by the Spirit of God, they are the sons of God.

For ye have not received the spirit of bondage again to fear; but ye have received the Spirit of adoption, whereby we cry, Abba, Father.

The Spirit itself beareth witness with our spirit, that we are the children of God:

And if children, then heirs; heirs of God, and joint-heirs with Christ; if so be that we suffer with him, that we may be also glorified together.

For I reckon that the sufferings of this present time are not worthy to be compared with the glory which shall be revealed in us.

For the earnest expectation of the creature waiteth for the manifestation of the sons of God.

For the creature was made subject to vanity, not willingly, but by reason of him who hath subjected the same in hope,

Because the creature itself also shall be delivered from the bondage of corruption into the glorious liberty of the children of God. . . .

For whom he did foreknow, he also did predestinate to be conformed to the image of his Son, that he might be the firstborn among many brethren.

—Romans 8:14–21, 29

But whoso shall offend one of these little ones which believe in me, it were better for him that a millstone were hanged about his neck, and that he were drowned in the depth of the sea. . . .

Take heed that ye despise not one of these little ones; for I say unto you, That in heaven their angels do always behold the face of my Father which is in heaven.

—Matthew 18:6, 10

But if we walk in the light, as he is in the light, we have fellowship one with another, and the blood of Jesus Christ his Son cleanseth us from all sin.

If we say that we have no sin, we deceive ourselves, and the truth is not in us.

If we confess our sins, he is faithful and just to forgive us our sins, and to cleanse us from all unrighteousness.

—1 John 1:7–9

For ye are bought with a price: therefore glorify God in your body, and in your spirit, which are God's.

—1 Corinthians 6:20

—Nine—

Let's Make This Marriage Work

You know you've made a lifelong commitment to make a go of it. Divorce is not an option. Every problem, every squabble, every major grief or minor concern must bend itself to this set-in-stone prior decision: We will pass through this thing intact and come out the other side. Still married. Still in love.

Yes, You Will Face Problems

In Thorton Wilder's play The Skin of Our Teeth, the character Mrs. Antrobus says to her husband, "I didn't marry you because you were perfect. . . . I married you because you gave me a promise." She takes off her ring and looks at it. "That promise made up for your faults, and the promise I gave you made up for mine. Two imperfect people got married, and it was the promise that made the marriage."

—*Anonymous*[1]

Beloved, think it not strange concerning the fiery trial which is to try you, as though some strange thing happened unto you:

But rejoice, inasmuch as ye are partakers of Christ's sufferings; that, when his glory shall be revealed, ye may be glad also with exceeding joy.

If ye be reproached for the name of Christ, happy are ye; for the spirit of glory and of God resteth upon you: on their part he is evil spoken of, but on your part he is glorified.

But let none of you suffer as a murderer, or as a thief, or as an evildoer, or as a busybody in other men's matters.

Yet if any man suffer as a Christian, let him not be ashamed; but let him glorify God on this behalf.

For the time is come that judgment must begin at the house of God: and if it first begin at us, what shall the end be of them that obey not the gospel of God?

And if the righteous scarcely be saved, where shall the ungodly and the sinner appear?

Wherefore let them that suffer according to the will of God commit the keeping of their souls to him in well doing, as unto a faithful Creator.

—1 Peter 4:12–19

Be sober, be vigilant; because your adversary the devil, as a roaring lion, walketh about, seeking whom he may devour.

—1 Peter 5:8

If the world hate you, ye know that it hated me before it hated you.

If ye were of the world, the world would love his own: but because ye are not of the world, but I have chosen you out of the world, therefore the world hateth you.

—John 15:18–19

Do the Right Things for a Healthy Marriage

The difficulty with marriage is that we fall in love with a personality, but must live with a character.

—Peter DeVries[2]

❤ *Follow Others' Example of Diligence*

Joash was minded to repair the house of the LORD.

And he gathered together the priest and the Levites, and said to them, Go out unto the cities of Judah, and gather of all Israel money to repair the house of your God from year to year, and see that ye hasten the matter. Howbeit the Levites hastened it not.

—2 Chronicles 24:4b–5

Now it came to pass upon a day, that Jonathan the son of Saul said unto the young man that bare his armour, Come, and let us go over to the Philistines' garrison, that is on the other side. But he told not his father. . . .

And Jonathan said to the young man that bare his armour, Come, and let us go over unto the garrison of these uncircumcised: it may be that the LORD will work for us: for there is no restraint to the LORD to save by many or by few.

And his armourbearer said unto him, Do all that is in thine heart: turn thee; behold, I am with thee according to thy heart.

—1 Samuel 14:1, 6–7

And Jesus arose, and followed him, and so did his disciples.

And, behold, a woman, which was diseased with an issue of blood twelve years, came behind him, and touched the hem of his garment:

For she said within herself, If I may but touch his garment, I shall be whole.

But Jesus turned him about, and when he saw her, he said, Daughter, be of good comfort; thy faith hath made thee whole. And the woman was made whole from that hour.

—Matthew 9:19–22

❤ *Seek God's Guidance in All Things*

For the LORD's portion is his people; Jacob is the lot of his inheritance.

He found him in a desert land, and in the waste howling wilderness; he led him about, he instructed him, he kept him as the apple of his eye.

As an eagle stirreth up her nest, fluttereth over her young, spreadeth abroad her wings, taketh them, beareth them on her wings:

So the LORD alone did lead him, and there was no strange god with him.

He made him ride on the high places of the earth, that he might eat the increase of the fields; and he made him to suck honey out of the rock, and oil out of the flinty rock;

Butter of kine, and milk of sheep, with fat of lambs, and rams of the breed of Bashan, and goats, with the fat of kidneys of wheat; and thou didst drink the pure blood of the grape.

—Deuteronomy 32:9–14

And I will bring the blind by a way that they knew not; I will lead them in paths that they have not known: I will make darkness light before them, and crooked things straight. These things will I do unto them, and not forsake them.

—Isaiah 42:16

Let not mercy and truth forsake thee: bind them about thy neck; write them upon the table of thine heart:

So shalt thou find favour and good understanding in the sight of God and man.

Trust in the Lord with all thine heart; and lean not unto thine own understanding.

In all thy ways acknowledge him, and he shall direct thy paths.

—Proverbs 3:3–6

For this God is our God for ever and ever: he will be our guide even unto death.

—Psalm 48:14

Teach me thy way, O Lord, and lead me in a plain path, because of mine enemies.

—Psalm 27:11

Lead me in thy truth, and teach me: for thou art the God of my salvation; on thee do I wait all the day.

Remember, O Lord, thy tender mercies and thy lovingkindnesses; for they have been ever of old.

Remember not the sins of my youth, nor my transgressions: according to thy mercy remember thou me for thy goodness' sake, O LORD.

Good and upright is the LORD: therefore will he teach sinners in the way.

The meek will he guide in judgment: and the meek will he teach his way.

—Psalm 25:5–9

I will instruct thee and teach thee in the way which thou shalt go: I will guide thee with mine eye.

—Psalm 32:8

❤ *Put on Perseverance*

Although the fig tree shall not blossom, neither shall fruit be in the vines; the labour of the olive shall fail, and the fields shall yield no meat; the flock shall be cut off from the fold, and there shall be no herd in the stalls:

Yet I will rejoice in the LORD, I will joy in the God of my salvation.

The LORD God is my strength, and he will make my feet like hinds' feet, and he will make me to walk upon mine high places. To the chief singer on my stringed instruments.

—*Habakkuk 3:17–19*

And whosoever doth not bear his cross, and come after me, cannot be my disciple.

For which of you, intending to build a tower, sitteth not down first, and counteth the cost, whether he have sufficient to finish it?

Lest haply, after he hath laid the foundation, and is not able to finish it, all that behold it begin to mock him,

Saying, This man began to build, and was not able to finish.

Or what king, going to make war against another king, sitteth not down first, and consulteth whether he be able with ten thousand to meet him that cometh against him with twenty thousand?

Or else, while the other is yet a great way off, he sendeth an ambassage, and desireth conditions of peace.

So likewise, whosoever he be of you that forsaketh not all that he hath, he cannot be my disciple.

Salt is good: but if the salt have lost his savour, wherewith shall it be seasoned?

It is neither fit for the land, nor yet for the dunghill; but men cast it out. He that hath ears to hear, let him hear.

—Luke 14:27–35

And let us not be weary in well doing: for in due season we shall reap, if we faint not.

—Galatians 6:9

For consider him that endured such contradiction of sinners against himself, lest ye be wearied and faint in your minds.

Ye have not yet resisted unto blood, striving against sin.

—Hebrews 12:3–4

Know ye not that they which run in a race run all, but one receiveth the prize? So run, that ye may obtain.

And every man that striveth for the mastery is temperate in all things. Now they do it to obtain a corruptible crown; but we an incorruptible.

I therefore so run, not as uncertainly; so fight I, not as one that beateth the air:

But I keep under my body, and bring it into subjection: lest that by any means, when I have preached to others, I myself should be a castaway.

—1 Corinthians 9:24–27

❤ *Renew Your Strength*

I will cry unto God most high; unto God that performeth all things for me.

He shall send from heaven, and save me from the reproach of him that would swallow me up. God shall send forth his mercy and his truth.

—Psalm 57:2–3

Wherefore lift up the hands which hang down, and the feeble knees;

And make straight paths for your feet, lest that which is lame be turned out of the way; but let it rather be healed.

Follow peace with all men, and holiness, without which no man shall see the Lord:

Looking diligently lest any man fail of the grace of God; lest any root of bitterness springing up trouble you, and thereby many be defiled.

—*Hebrews 12:12–15*

Blessed are they that mourn: for they shall be comforted.

Blessed are the meek: for they shall inherit the earth.

Blessed are they which do hunger and thirst after righteousness: for they shall be filled.

Blessed are the merciful: for they shall obtain mercy.

Blessed are the pure in heart: for they shall see God.

Blessed are the peacemakers: for they shall be called the children of God.

Blessed are they which are persecuted for righteousness' sake: for theirs is the kingdom of heaven.

—*Matthew 5:4–10*

Behold, the Lord GOD will help me; who is he that shall condemn me? lo, they all shall wax old as a garment; the moth shall eat them up.

Who is among you that feareth the LORD, that obeyeth the voice of his servant, that walketh in darkness, and hath no light? let him trust in the name of the LORD, and stay upon his God.

—Isaiah 50:9–10

For thou hast delivered my soul from death: wilt not thou deliver my feet from falling, that I may walk before God in the light of the living?

—Psalm 56:13

❤ *Stay Trustworthy*

Blessed is the man whom thou choosest, and causest to approach unto thee, that he may dwell in thy courts: we shall be satisfied with the goodness of thy house, even of thy holy temple.

—Psalm 65:4

For the grace of God that bringeth salvation hath appeared to all men,

Teaching us that, denying ungodliness and worldly lusts, we should live soberly, righteously, and godly, in this present world.

—*Titus 2:11–12*

They that are Christ's have crucified the flesh with the affections and lusts.

—*Galatians 5:24*

Therefore, brethren, we are debtors, not to the flesh, to live after the flesh.

For if ye live after the flesh, ye shall die: but if ye through the Spirit do mortify the deeds of the body, ye shall live.

—*Romans 8:12–13*

❤ *Maintain Strong Values*

And Moses called unto Joshua, and said unto him in the sight of all Israel, Be strong and of a good courage: for thou must go with this people unto the land which the LORD hath sworn unto their fathers to give them; and thou shalt cause them to inherit it.

And the LORD, he it is that doth go before thee; he will be with thee, he will not fail thee, neither forsake thee: fear not, neither be dismayed.

—Deuteronomy 31:7–8

If ye then be risen with Christ, seek those things which are above, where Christ sitteth on the right hand of God.

Set your affection on things above, not on things on the earth.

For ye are dead, and your life is hid with Christ in God.

When Christ, who is our life, shall appear, then shall ye also appear with him in glory.

Mortify therefore your members which are upon the earth; fornication, uncleanness, inordinate affection, evil concupiscence, and covetousness, which is idolatry:

For which things' sake the wrath of God cometh on the children of disobedience.

—Colossians 3:1–6

If we live in the Spirit, let us also walk in the Spirit.

Let us not be desirous of vain glory, provoking one another, envying one another.

—Galatians 5:25–26

And be not conformed to this world: but be ye transformed by the renewing of your mind, that ye may prove what is that good, and acceptable, and perfect, will of God.

—Romans 12:2

Love not the world, neither the things that are in the world. If any man love the world, the love of the Father is not in him.

For all that is in the world, the lust of the flesh, and the lust of the eyes, and the pride of life, is not of the Father, but is of the world.

And the world passeth away, and the lust thereof: but he that doeth the will of God abideth for ever.

—1 John 2:15–17

❤ *Stay Dedicated*

And when they had ordained them elders in every church, and had prayed with fasting, they commended them to the Lord, on whom they believed.

And after they had passed throughout Pisidia, they came to Pamphylia.

And when they had preached the word in Perga, they went down into Attalia:

And thence sailed to Antioch, from whence they had been recommended to the grace of God for the work which they fulfilled.

—Acts 14:23–26

Commit thy way unto the LORD; trust also in him; and he shall bring it to pass.

—Psalm 37:5

Are they ministers of Christ? (I speak as a fool) I am more; in labours more abundant, in stripes above measure, in prisons more frequent, in deaths oft.

Of the Jews five times received I forty stripes save one.

Thrice was I beaten with rods, once was I stoned, thrice I suffered shipwreck, a night and a day I have been in the deep;

In journeyings often, in perils of waters, in perils of robbers, in perils by mine own countrymen, in perils by the heathen, in perils in the city, in perils in the wilderness, in perils in the sea, in perils among false brethren;

In weariness and painfulness, in watchings often, in hunger and thirst, in fastings often, in cold and nakedness.

Beside those things that are without, that which cometh upon me daily, the care of all the churches.

Who is weak, and I am not weak? who is offended, and I burn not?

If I must needs glory, I will glory of the things which concern mine infirmities.

The God and Father of our Lord Jesus Christ, which is blessed for evermore, knoweth that I lie not.

—2 Corinthians 11:23–31

❤ *Confront Your Fears*

Have mercy upon me, O LORD, for I am in trouble: mine eye is consumed with grief, yea, my soul and my belly.

For my life is spent with grief, and my years with sighing: my strength faileth because of mine iniquity, and my bones are consumed.

I was a reproach among all mine enemies, but especially among my neighbours, and a fear to mine acquaintance: they that did see me without fled from me.

I am forgotten as a dead man out of mind: I am like a broken vessel.

For I have heard the slander of many: fear was on every side: while they took counsel together against me, they devised to take away my life.

—Psalm 31:9–13

Be strong and of a good courage, fear not, nor be afraid of them: for the LORD thy God, he it is that doth go with thee; he will not fail thee, nor forsake thee.

—Deuteronomy 31:6

Have not I commanded thee? Be strong and of a good courage; be not afraid, neither be thou dismayed: for the LORD thy God is with thee whithersoever thou goest.

—Joshua 1:9

Though an host should encamp against me, my heart shall not fear: though war should rise against me, in this will I be confident.

—Psalm 27:3

There is no fear in love; but perfect love casteth out fear: because fear hath torment. He that feareth is not made perfect in love.

—1 John 4:18

For God hath not given us the spirit of fear; but of power, and of love, and of a sound mind.

—2 Timothy 1:7

Notes

Chapter 2

1. Samuel Goodrich, quoted in *Correct Quotes* (Sausalito, CA: Wordstar International, Inc. 1991).
2. David LaPlaca, in *It Happened after the Honeymoon* (Wheaton, IL: Harold Shaw Publishers, 1994).
3. Sydney Smith, *Correct Quotes*
4. Penny Bilofsky and Fredda Sacharow, in *Couples' Devotional Bible*, edited by the staff of *Marriage Partnership* magazine (Grand Rapids, MI: Zondervan, 1994).
5. Gary Wilde, *Simple Prayers and Blessings* (Lincolnwood, IL: Publications International, 1998).

Chapter 3

1. Gary Wilde, *Simple Prayers and Blessings*

Chapter 4

1. David Augsburger, *Caring Enough to Confront* (Glendale, CA: GL / Regal Books, 1976).
2. Gary Wilde, *Simple Prayers and Blessings*
3. John Powell, in *The Secret of Staying in Love.*

4. Peter Ustinov, quoted in "Points to Ponder," *Reader's Digest*, Oct. 1992.
5. G. K. Chesterton, in *Quotations for the Soul*, op. cit.

Chapter 5

1. Quoted in James Hewett, ed., *Illustrations Unlimited* (Wheaton, IL: Tyndale, 1988).

Chapter 6

1. J. I. Packer, in *Your Father Loves You.*
2. David and Vera Mace, *It Happened after the Honeymoon*
3. Carole Streeter, in *Finding Your Place After Divorce.*

Chapter 7

1. Gary Wilde, *Simple Prayers and Blessings*
2. Wilde, Ibid.

Chapter 8

1. Pablo Casals, quoted in Jack Canfield, *Chicken Soup for the Soul* (Deerfield Beach, FL: Health Communications, 1996).
2. Ellen Goodman, *Boston Globe*, quoted on the Internet, at Illustration Research Service, www.IRSweb.com.

Chapter 9

1. Quoted in James Hewett, ed., *Illustrations Unlimited*
2. Peter DeVries, *Correct Quotes*